DOCAT

What to do?
The Social Teaching
of the Catholic Church

STUDY GUIDE

IGNATIUS PRESS - AUGUSTINE INSTITUTE
SAN FRANCISCO, CA   GREENWOOD VILLAGE, CO

Nihil Obstat: Dr. Jared Staudt, B.A., M.A., Ph.D., *Censor Deputatus*
Imprimatur: Most Rev. Samuel J. Aquila, S.T.L., Archbishop of Denver,
Colorado, USA, June 20, 2016

Use of the cover design and logo of DOCAT with kind permission of the
YOUCAT Foundation gGmbH, Königstein/Ts., Germany. YOUCAT® is an
internationally registered and protected brand name and logo. Filed under
GM: 011929131 Design, layout, illustrations: Alexander von Lengerke,
Cologne, Germany.

Writer: Ashley Crane.
Print Production/Graphic Design: Jeff Cole, Ann Diaz, Christina Gray,
Brenda Kraft, Devin Schadt.

Ignatius Press Distribution
P.O. Box 1339
Fort Collins, CO 80522
Tel: (800) 651-1531
www.ignatius.com

Augustine Institute
6160 South Syracuse Way, Suite 310
Greenwood Village, CO 80111
Tel: (866) 767-3155
www.AugustineInstitute.org

Printed in the United States of America
ISBN: 978-1-62164-136-0

TABLE OF CONTENTS

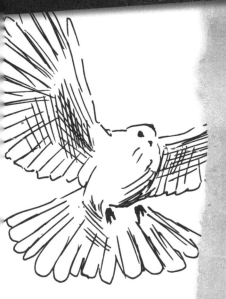

INTRODUCTION ———
WELCOME TO THE DOCAT STUDY GUIDE

The social doctrine of the Catholic Church contains a wealth of resources for how to live out the faith in pursuit of charity and justice. DOCAT presents this social doctrine of the Church in a way designed specifically for young adults, helping you to respond effectively to Pope Francis's challenge to work for greater justice in the world.

Based on the *Catechism of the Catholic Church* and other important Church documents, DOCAT is written in a style and format just for you. Through probing questions and thought-provoking exercises, DOCAT teaches how to understand and joyfully live according to the principles of truth, justice, and charity set forth in the social doctrine of the Church.

The truths of the faith are not meant to be merely an intellectual exercise—they are meant to make a real, tangible difference in daily life. As Jesus tells his Apostles at the Last Supper, **"By this all men will know that you are my disciples, if you have love for one another"** (John 13:35).

What does this love look like? It is loving your neighbor as yourself and praying for those who persecute you (*cf.* Matthew 5:44). It is giving food to the hungry and drink to the thirsty, welcoming the stranger, clothing the naked, and visiting the sick and imprisoned. Love of God cannot be separated from service to others because when you care for others, you are serving God (*cf.* Matthew 25:34–40).

Translated into multiple languages and distributed throughout the world, DOCAT can have a profound effect on young Catholics everywhere. By learning to live a life transformed by God's love, we can then, in turn, transform the world.

HOW TO USE THE STUDY GUIDE

The *Study Guide* is divided into the same twelve parts as DOCAT, which reflect twelve important categories of Catholic social doctrine. Though the parts can be studied in any order, it is best to let the *Study Guide* lead you through DOCAT by starting at the beginning.

The twelve sections of DOCAT and this *Study Guide* explain what the Church teaches about the dignity of the human person and what that means for all areas of life, from the family to the international community to economics, politics, and the environment. For each of these sections, the *Study Guide* has three topics for study, discussion, further reflection, and application in your daily life.

You'll find the same format for each topic. First you'll dive into DOCAT, starting with a brief introduction to the topic (Behind DOCAT), followed by a reading assignment (Read DOCAT) and short-answer questions (What Does DOCAT Say?). You'll notice that in the numbered paragraphs and along the margins of DOCAT are quotations from the Bible. To help you read and reflect on these, we've included questions about those passages, as well as some other important Bible texts (What Does the Bible Say?). Next, you'll find some questions to reflect on, either independently or as a group (DO Reflect), followed by discussion questions for either large or small groups (DO Chat). Finally, we've provided some tasks for you to do in the coming week to help you apply what you've learned (DO Challenge).

PART 1

GOD'S MASTER PLAN: LOVE

▶ "The world is created for
the honor of God."

—Vatican Council I

TOPIC 1 | **GOD IS LOVE**

▶ Behind DOCAT

Who is God, and how are we supposed to relate to him? If we don't get this fundamental question right, we won't get anything else right either. In order to understand our role in this world and know how to relate to others in truth and love, we must first understand who God is and what that says about our own identity and purpose.

▶ Read DOCAT

Read nos. 1–5.

▶ What Does DOCAT Say?

1. What is the "red thread running through God's creation," according to no. 1? What does this tell us about God's plan of creation?

2. According to no. 3, how can we recognize what good actions are?

3. Why did God create us?

▶ What Does the Bible Say?

1. How does 1 John 4:7–12 explain the relationship between loving God and loving others?

2. Read Matthew 5:43–48. By what standard are we supposed to measure our lives? What are the criteria?

God created this world because of his great love. He is the origin, cause, and goal of all things that exist. This means that God cares about everything—nothing is too small for his notice. So every moment of our lives, every decision that we make, every thought that we have matters to God. Not because he is some control-freak who just won't leave us alone but because he loves us! And God wants us to love him in return because he created us to love him, and so, he knows that loving him is what is going to make us truly happy. Yes, God really does want us to be happy. And the path to true happiness is love.

1 Do you believe that God cares about every detail of your life? What difference does it make whether he does or doesn't?

2 Do you believe God created everything because of love? If not, why else would God create the world and all that is in it?

3 What do you think the purpose of all of creation is? What do you think your purpose in life is?

DO Chat

1. What are some things that make it difficult to follow God's plan for us to "think, speak, and act in love" (no. 1)?

2. How does God's love for you affect how you treat others?

DO Challenge

Remember: Remind yourself each day this week that all of creation comes from and is destined to return to God's love.

Thank and Ask: Spend time in prayer thanking God for his great love, and ask him how you can better show that love to the people around you.

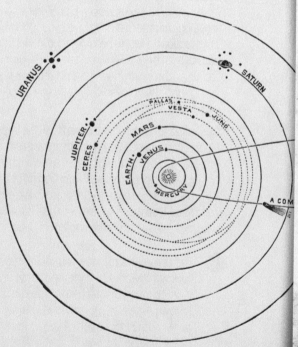

NOTES

▶ Behind DOCAT

When asked the question, "What's wrong with the world today?" the famous G.K. Chesterton is reported to have answered quite simply, "I am."

There is certainly something wrong with our world. Somewhere between God creating everything and declaring that it was "very good" (Genesis 1:31) and the present, something has clearly gone very wrong. That something is sin. From the moment Adam and Eve ate the forbidden fruit in the Garden, evil entered the world and has been wreaking havoc ever since. But the brokenness in our world today isn't due to that first sin alone—every sin committed contributes to it. Do we, like Chesterton, acknowledge some responsibility for the problems created by sin?

The good news is we aren't stuck with the status quo. What do we need to fix this broken world? All we need is love! God has fully revealed his love to us in Jesus Christ, and through the grace of the sacraments he enables us to work toward a civilization of love. By choosing to act in love, we can help heal the wounds caused by sin.

▶ Read DOCAT

Read nos. 6–14.

▶ What Does DOCAT Say?

1. How can we explain the presence of evil in a world that God created as something good?

2. What is the relationship between love and freedom?

3. According to no. 12, what are the basic rules of life together in society?

4. What is the beginning of the civilization of love?

DO reflect

"Do unto others as you would have them do unto you." "Love your neighbor as yourself" (Mark 12:31). The Golden Rule and the second greatest commandment. You have probably heard them over and over again. On the surface they seem so simple—treat others the way you want to be treated. It isn't always easy in practice. As if it weren't enough of a challenge just to love others as we love ourselves, Jesus gives us a new and even greater commandment: "Love one another as I have loved you" (John 15:12). The standard of loving behavior is no longer just natural human love—now the standard is divine love. Treating others with kindness and fairness is replaced with loving the unlovable more than we love our own lives.

God asks a lot of us, but he doesn't ask the impossible. He doesn't expect us to do anything he hasn't already done for us, and he doesn't ask us to do anything on our own strength alone. When God gives us a command, he also gives us the grace to live out that command. God wants to use us to heal the world with love. All we have to do is follow his lead.

 The command to "love your neighbor as yourself" (Mark 12:31) means that you have to love yourself before you can truly love anyone else. Do you love yourself? Why or why not? How might a lack of love for oneself get in the way of loving others?

 What does it mean to love others as Jesus has loved us? What do you think this should look like in your own life?

3 None of us can do this alone. What steps can you take to be strengthened in God's love in order to share that love with those around you?

▶ What Does the Bible Say?

1. Read 1 Corinthians 13:4–8. What does this passage reveal about how God loves us?

2. Look up Leviticus 19:18 and John 15:12. How is Jesus's commandment similar to the Old Law? How is it new?

DO Chat

1. Why does God's revelation of himself demand a response? Or to put it another way: Why can't we just continue on as we were before we knew God?

2. If the Ten Commandments were already written on the human heart as natural law (no. 12), why do you think God also gave them to Moses at Mount Sinai?

3. How does our love for others heal the wounds sin has caused in the world?

DO Challenge

Memorize and Reflect: If you haven't already, memorize the Ten Commandments. Which commandment do you need to work harder at remembering and obeying?

Remember: Remind yourself each day this week that God loves you profoundly and that your love for others has its source in God's love for you.

NOTES

▶ Behind DOCAT

Mankind was designed with a longing for the perfect and the eternal. As Ecclesiastes says, "[God] has put eternity into man's mind" (Ecclesiastes 3:11). We are created for Heaven, but we are living on a very imperfect earth. Even people who have no faith in God or no expectation of an afterlife recognize that the world in which we live is not perfect and desire to make it better. Since we were designed this way, it makes sense that we would be dissatisfied with the broken state of the world and want to fix it.

By working for a more just and loving society, we are working to bring this world into conformity with the Kingdom of God. Jesus said that the Kingdom of God was like a mustard seed—something tiny that grows into something huge (*cf.* Matthew 13:31–32). The Church is Christ's kingly reign on earth, changing this world broken by sin and death into the fullness of the Kingdom of God. And while we hope to achieve a revolution of love in our world today, this process is truly a journey into eternity because the full transformation will be realized only in Heaven.

▶ Read DOCAT

Read nos. 15–21.

▶ What Does DOCAT Say?

1. According to no. 15, what is the only way we can succeed in living a life of love?

2. What is at the core of every human sin?

3. Why does the Church exist?

DO reflect

Sometimes when we are working very hard on something important, we can become so wrapped up in the task at hand that we lose sight of the bigger picture. We need to be aware of this temptation when we are striving for a better world here on earth. Working for justice and peace is an incredibly important job, but it is not the final goal. Everything we do here on earth should be driven by our hope of eternal life. St. Augustine put this in terms of an earthly city and a heavenly city. While we rightly strive to improve the earthly city—our human society—to the best of our abilities, we remember that it will ultimately pass away while the perfect heavenly city endures. If we lose sight of our end goal—Heaven—we will fail to make real progress in love and justice on earth. The Church keeps us focused on the big picture while also providing the means to do the necessary work here on earth.

1. Why is our hope for eternal life significant to the way we work to make a better world here?

2. Through the sacraments, God gives us the strength to improve the earthly city. What are some ways that you can put into practice the love you receive in the sacraments?

▶ What Does the Bible Say?

1. According to John 15:13, what is the greatest love a person can have? How do you think you can live this out in your own life?

2. Read Acts 2:44–45. How did inner conversion affect the outward actions of the early Christians in Jerusalem?

3. In 1 Corinthians 12, St. Paul talks about the Church as the Body of Christ. What does 1 Corinthians 12:26 tell us about our relationship and responsibility to other members of the Church?

DO Chat

1. What does it mean that love is not just a feeling but also a virtue? How is this similar to or different from the way the world commonly looks at love?

2. We cannot change the world without experiencing change (conversion) in our own hearts. How can we work on changing ourselves to get ready to change the world?

3. How does the Church help us develop in God's love?

DO Challenge

Remember: At your Baptism, you became a member of the Body of Christ, the Church. Make a plan for celebrating the anniversary of your Baptism and mark the date on the calendar so you remember.

Pray: The next time you go to Mass and receive the Eucharist, ask our Lord how he wants his love to transform your actions in the coming week.

NOTES

NOTES

PART 2

TOGETHER WE ARE STRONG: THE CHURCH'S SOCIAL MISSION

"Do all the good you can, by all the means you can, in all the ways you can, in all the places you can, at all the times you can, to all the people you can, as long as ever you can."

—John Wesley (1703–1791), known as "John Wesley's Rule"

TOPIC 1 | SOCIAL BUTTERFLIES

▶ Behind DOCAT

We all know someone who loves to be around people constantly. Whether it's hanging out with a group of friends or meeting new people, these "social butterflies" flit from one interaction to another, happy to be constantly encountering and relating to other people. Maybe this is you, or maybe you don't love being around other people all the time. But whether you are an extrovert thriving on being around other people or an introvert needing some solitude to recharge, you are most certainly a social creature. All of us are created for community because we are created in the image and likeness of the Triune God, who is himself a community of Persons.

It is not only our human nature but also our vocation as Christians that makes us social. The Church is a community—even more than that, the Church is the Body of Christ. And so while we maintain our individuality, we do so as members of something larger than ourselves. This connects us in a very real way with every other member of the Body. This deep and abiding connection is at the heart of the social mission of the Church.

▶ Read DOCAT

Read nos. 22–27.

▶ What Does DOCAT Say?

1. What are the two purposes of social doctrine?

2. To what does the term "social doctrine" refer?

3. According to no. 26, is God (and therefore his Church) interested in the individual or the community?

▶ DO reflect

We are created for relationship with one another and ultimately with God. That means we aren't expected to get through life on our own. Of course, no matter what you face, God is with us. But even with that encouragement, we may sometimes find ourselves wishing we could see and feel and hear God at our side. This is one of the reasons Jesus gave us the Church—to be the community that we need to help us through this life and to get us to Heaven. This is a huge gift! It means we have not only our friends and family as our community, but also our parish, the whole Church here on earth, as well as the entire communion of saints in Heaven. Talk about a great community! But membership in the Body of Christ comes with responsibility as well. Just as other members of the body will help us along the way, we also need to offer our love and prayers in the service of others. This is the shape of the journey: you, Christ, and the rest of the Church. As Ecclesiastes 4:12 says, "A threefold cord is not quickly broken."

1. In what ways do you most need the help of the Church?

2. What are some ways that you live out your responsibility to other members of the Body of Christ?

3. Why is it important that the Church is a tangible, visible community and not just a spiritual reality?

▶ What Does the Bible Say?

1. Throughout the account of creation, God declares over and over that "it is good." According to Genesis 2:18, what is the first thing that is "not good" in creation? Why do you think this situation is not good?

2. What does Psalm 139 have to say about God's concern for you as an individual?

3. Read Revelation 21:2–3. The "holy city, new Jerusalem" in Revelation is the Church. What does this passage tell us about the relationship between God, the Church, and us?

DO Chat

1. Why do you think the Christian concept of the dignity of the human person is a necessary foundation for a free and just social order?

2. What are some of the signs of the times, the urgent social questions of our world today?

3. No. 24 says that "all members of the Church... participate in the development of social doctrine." What are some things you can do to participate in the development of social doctrine?

DO Challenge

Think and Thank: On whom do you rely the most in your daily life? Make a point this week of thanking that person for his or her support. Who relies on you? Think of a way that you can be an even greater support to that person this week.

Pray: Ask God how you can strengthen your bond with other members of the Body of Christ.

NOTES

TOPIC 2
FAITH AND JUSTICE

▶ **Behind DOCAT**

The spiritual mission of the Church is pretty obvious: to get people to Heaven. But the Church also cares about the physical and emotional well-being of her children and not just their spiritual health. The human person is body and soul, and the Church cares for both. This is why the social doctrine of the Church is so important. Making a better world here and now goes hand in hand with our heavenly destiny. To be a Christian means caring that others are fed both spiritually and physically. There are many ways to do this, and so the Church puts forth guidelines and principles in her social teaching, and it is up to us to put those into practice.

▶ **Read DOCAT**

Read nos. 28–36.

▶ **What Does DOCAT Say?**

1. According to no. 30, what is the relationship between development aid and the proclamation of the faith?

2. What basic characteristics must a political or societal model have for the Church to approve it?

3. Why does the Church speak out on social questions?

DO reflect

The Church does not create political policies or tell society what exactly to do to solve individual problems. It is the job of the individual Christian, especially the lay Christian, to be involved in politics and specific social causes. This means that you are called to work toward building that city of man "in greater conformity with the Kingdom of God" (*Compendium of Social Doctrine*, 63). There are many ways to do this, and each of us answers this call according to our own unique gifts and opportunities. How we put the principles of the Church's social doctrine into concrete practice will be somewhat different for each one of us, but we must all get involved!

 Which social problem(s) do you feel most strongly about? Why?

 What talents do you have that could help you work toward a solution to that problem?

▶ What Does the Bible Say?

1. How does the analogy of yeast leavening dough in Matthew 13:33 shed light on the way Christians should work in society?

2. Read Mark 12:17. What do you owe to God? What do you owe to Caesar (the government or society in general)? Do you think your duty to God and your duty to society are ever in conflict? Why or why not?

3. Read the description of true religion in James 1:27. St. Thomas Aquinas explained that some acts of religion are focused on God directly (such as sacrifice and prayer), while other acts of religion honor God by obeying his commands. Why do you think both of these kinds of acts are necessary for true religion?

DO Chat

1. As the hands and feet of Christ, what can we do to get involved in politics? What can others do to be involved in the political process even if they aren't old enough to vote?

2. What would you say to someone who claims that the Church has no right to speak out about the problems of a secular society?

DO Challenge

Pray: Take some time each day this week to pray for your elected officials.

Seek: Ask God how he wants you to be more involved in working for a better society.

Act: If you are old enough to vote, make sure you are registered with your current address.

NOTES

▶ **Behind DOCAT**

When is the last time you went an entire day—a whole 24 hours—without being exposed to any kind of media? No TV or movies, no Internet, no social networking sites, no computer games. Can you remember? What was it like?

We rely very heavily on new media. We use it for education and communication as well as for entertainment. This technology has enormous potential for good, but we must be mindful of how we use it. New media makes an excellent servant but a poor master.

▶ **Read DOCAT**

Read nos. 37–46.

▶ **What Does DOCAT Say?**

1. What is the ethical responsibility of the media (and those who make it available and distribute it)?

2. What is the responsibility of one using media?

3. Is media inherently good? If so, does this mean its use is always good?

DO reflect

The new media is an amazing and effective tool, providing an unprecedented opportunity for communication and collaboration. But, like any powerful tool, media comes with risks if not used responsibly. New media—and particularly social media—allows for the creation of communities with practically no borders or limits. However, this type of communication can actually weaken interpersonal connections if used indiscriminately. We can communicate with anyone in the world instantaneously, but we can also hide behind our screens and forget that there is a real person deserving of our love and respect on the other end. Uncharitable words that may seem too harsh to speak in person flow easily over the Internet. And in a world of memes and sound bites, it can be difficult to preserve true, respectful dialogue.

 In what ways do you think new media enhances interpersonal connections? In what ways can it weaken relationships?

 How can you fulfill Christ's command to love your neighbor as yourself when using new media? Do you think this is easier or more difficult than in face-to-face communication? Why?

▶ What Does the Bible Say?

1. Read Ephesians 4:15–16 and 29–30. According to St. Paul, how are we to speak to one another? Why is it so important for us to speak this way?

2. In his letter, St. James points out how powerful the tongue (speech) is and how dangerous it can be when used in an unloving way. According to James 3:8–10, what is especially unfitting about speaking without love?

3. How does Proverbs 15:1 advise you to respond to someone who disagrees with you?

4. What does Sirach 20:7 have to say about when to speak and when to be silent?

DO Chat

1. In order to serve the common good, communication on social networks should take the form of a dialogue—a conversation where there is a back-and-forth of ideas. In your experience, is it easy or difficult to use social media for a dialogue? Why? What steps can you take to encourage dialogue on social media?

2. What do you think it means to use media sensibly? What are some of the challenges to doing so, and how can you overcome them?

DO Challenge

Remember: Every time you use social media this week, remind yourself of your responsibility to God and to neighbor. Before you comment on or post anything, ask yourself if doing so serves both truth and charity.

Share: Using whichever form of media you prefer, share something that contributes to the common good—an uplifting quote, a Bible verse, a positive story, etc.

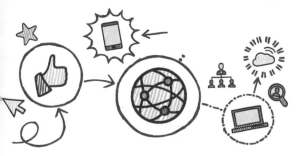

NOTES

NOTES

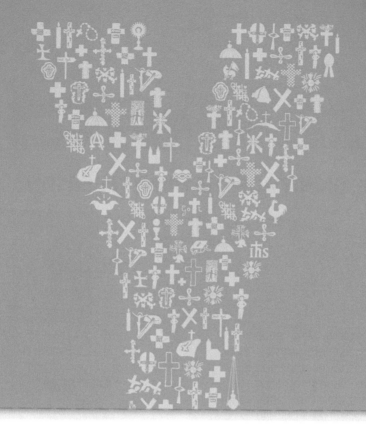

PART 3

UNIQUE AND INFINITELY VALUABLE: THE HUMAN PERSON

▶ "Then God said, 'Let us make man in our image, after our likeness...' So God created man in his own image, in the image of God he created him; male and female he created them."

—Genesis 1:26-27

TOPIC 1 | THE DIGNITY OF THE HUMAN PERSON

▶ **Behind DOCAT**

We spend a lot of time talking about groups of people—different communities, age groups, ethnic groups, religious groups, the poor, the sick, etc. But we can't forget that these groups are made up of individual persons. Most importantly, each individual person is made in the image and likeness of God, and therefore each person has equal, inviolable dignity. The dignity of the human person is the basis for all of the Church's social teaching. All of the rights, freedoms, and responsibilities of the human person are rooted in that God-given dignity.

▶ **Read DOCAT**

Read nos. 47–62.

▶ **What Does DOCAT Say?**

1. According to no. 51, what are the two dimensions of every sin?

2. What does the Church mean by the unity of the human person?

3. What is the goal or purpose of man's freedom?

▶ DO reflect

A lot of pop psychology focuses on "finding yourself." To find myself, I need to understand my emotions and motivations, accept myself for who I am, live up to my full potential, and so on. Do you see a theme here? It's all "me, me, me!"

The Church offers a different approach to fulfillment, and it's something we can't accomplish all alone. It's all about loving one another as God has loved us. Vatican II's *Gaudium et Spes* says that the "likeness between the union of the divine Persons," and the unity of God's sons in truth and charity...reveals that man, who is the only creature on earth that God willed for itself, cannot fully find himself except through a sincere gift of himself" (no. 24). God is a Trinity of Persons, a community of love. Since we are created in his image and likeness, we cannot find fulfillment without learning to give ourselves to others in love.

① Do you think that understanding our identity as children of God is an important step to loving others? Why or why not?

② Does being in community lead us closer to ourselves? What does it mean to be closer to yourself?

③ Think of all the communities of which you are a part. What principle of unity unites you with each of these communities? How does each community help shape you into who you are?

▶ What Does the Bible Say?

1. According to 1 John 3:1–2, what makes us children of God?

2. What does 1 Corinthians 3:16–17 teach us about how we should treat ourselves and others?

3. Read 1 Corinthians 6:12. What do you think St. Paul is saying about freedom? What kinds of things might be "lawful" but not "helpful"?

DO Chat

1. Do you think that it is important to recognize and respect your own dignity before you can recognize and respect the dignity of others? Why or why not?

2. No. 51 says, "To recognize and to name the sin is the first step in freeing oneself from it." What does this mean? What does this look like practically?

3. In what ways (if any) are men and women the same? In what ways (if any) are they different?

4. If we do not train our conscience properly, it will not be a trustworthy guide for our choices. What are some ways a person might fail to train his or her conscience? What can you do to form your conscience well?

DO Challenge

Reach Out: Who do you know who might be feeling isolated or excluded? Find a way to reach out to them to acknowledge their dignity and help them find an experience of community.

Learn: Choose one or two of the ways to form your conscience discussed in DO Chat no. 4 and work on forming your conscience this week.

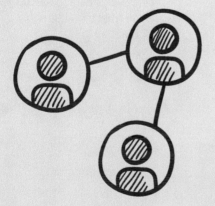

NOTES

HUMAN RIGHTS

▶ Behind DOCAT

On December 10, 1948, the United Nations General Assembly voted to accept the Universal Declaration of Human Rights. After the horrors and injustices of World War II, the international community wanted to provide for greater protection of the rights of all peoples. These rights are called "human rights" because they are not honors won by personal merit or privileges awarded by a government—they are rights that belong to each person simply because we are human, created in the image and likeness of God.

The first article of the Declaration states, "All human beings are born free and equal in dignity and rights. They are endowed with reason and conscience and should act towards one another in a spirit of brotherhood." Our rights have their foundation in our dignity, which stems from being persons made in the image and likeness of God. They also come with responsibilities, including the duty to speak up for and protect the rights of others.

▶ Read DOCAT

Read nos. 63–68.

▶ What Does DOCAT Say?

1. What are human rights, and what are their relationship to laws?

2. What is the fundamental human right? What are some other examples of important human rights?

DO reflect

The idea of "duty" sometimes has a negative connotation—it's a job we have to do, whether we want to or not. But if our rights come from our inherent dignity as human persons, then our duties are inscribed in our human nature as well. Scripture tells us what it means to live our lives according to the dignity we have as children of God, and the first two "duties" we have are the two greatest commandments: to love God and to love our neighbors. These duties aren't tiresome burdens distracting us from our own interests— they are what we were created to do. We aren't living up to our full potential if we ignore the duties that come along with the rights we want to claim. As Pope St. John XXIII said, "To claim one's rights and ignore one's duties, or only half fulfill them, is like building a house with one hand and tearing it down with the other."

 1 What do you think happens when a person claims his human rights without fulfilling the duties that come along with them?

2 What right is most important to you personally? What duties do you assume when embracing this right?

▶ What Does the Bible Say?

1. Proverbs 31 records the advice a mother gives to her son who is to be king. Read verses 8–9. How is someone with power and authority supposed to treat those in need?

2. Read Psalm 82:3–4 and Isaiah 1:17. What do these passages tell us about how God wants us to act?

DO Chat

1. We live in a society that often emphasizes rights and downplays responsibilities. How can you encourage others to fulfill their duties and not just exercise their rights?

2. What human rights do you think are most in danger of being denied or ignored in your own community? What needs to be done to protect these rights? What can you do?

DO Challenge

Read: Go online to http://www.un.org/en/universal-declaration-human-rights/ and read the Universal Declaration of Human Rights.

Thank and Ask: Make a list of the rights for which you are most thankful. Thank God for endowing you with these rights and ask him how you can better fulfill the responsibilities that accompany them.

Pray: Offer some sacrifice (go a day without eating meat, give up listening to music for a day, etc.) as a prayer for those whose human rights are not protected.

NOTES

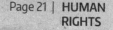

▶ **Behind DOCAT**

In the twentieth century, somewhere between 300 and 500 million people died of smallpox, an infectious disease causing flu-like symptoms followed by a rash of blisters covering most of the body. In 1980 it was confirmed that the disease had been completely eradicated due to a vigorous global vaccination campaign. Scientific advances in medicine led to an understanding of this disease and how to prevent it effectively through vaccination. Thanks to technology, a virus that used to be one of the leading causes of death now exists only in a few select laboratories.

Science can do amazing things to improve our quality of life, but it can also be misused. Just because we can do something doesn't mean that we should do it. Along with advances in science and technology come new questions about ethics: What is the right way to apply our newfound knowledge and capabilities? The dignity of the human person must always be taken into consideration; no matter how good the intentions, nothing that violates this dignity can be considered ethical.

▶ **Read DOCAT**

Read nos. 69–83.

▶ **What Does DOCAT Say?**

1. What kinds of questions are covered under the term "bioethics"?

2. When does human life begin? Is there a difference between the beginning of human life and the beginning of human personhood?

3. When is a person's dignity, right to life, and personal integrity particularly at risk?

4. Why is it not morally permissible to choose to end your own life?

DO reflect

The dignity of the human person is unconditional—it does not depend on age, ability, health, or anything else about a person. This means that all lives matter, regardless of what we might think the quality of that life is. From the moment of conception to the moment of natural death, a person's life, dignity, and bodily integrity must be protected as his most basic rights, from which all other rights stem.

The Church's social teaching is comprehensively pro-life. As St. John Paul II states, "The inviolability of the person which is a reflection of the absolute inviolability of God, finds its primary and fundamental expression in the inviolability of human life: for example, the right to health, to home, to work, to family, to culture—is false and illusory if the right to life, the most basic and fundamental right and the condition for all other personal rights, is not defended with maximum determination" (*Christifideles Laici*, 38). Therefore, we are called to speak up for and protect the right to life and the dignity of others at all stages of life. This means fighting for the rights of the unborn as well as providing love and support for pregnant mothers who find themselves in a difficult situation. It means being a voice for those suffering from domestic violence, feeding the hungry, praying for peace in war-torn countries, and protecting the sick and the elderly from the threat of euthanasia.

1 How would you define what it is means to be "pro-life"?

2 Do you think God is calling you personally to work for the protection of the dignity of human life? If so, in what way and at what stage of life? If not, why not?

▶ What Does the Bible Say?

1. What does Genesis 9:5–6 say about the consequences of taking a human life? Why is human life valuable, according to this passage?

2. It can be very hard to witness someone's suffering and not be able to do anything to stop it. Read 2 Corinthians 1:3–7. What does St. Paul have to say about what to do when confronted with suffering and afflictions?

3. First Peter 4:1 draws a connection between physical suffering and spiritual growth. Do you believe that God can bring a greater good out of suffering? Have you ever witnessed this or experienced it for yourself?

DO Chat

1. Do you believe that every human life has equal value and dignity? Why or why not?

2. What are some ways to reach out to someone who is suffering?

3. Abortion and euthanasia can both be very emotionally charged topics. What do you think you should do to share your beliefs in a charitable way? What should you avoid?

DO Challenge

Resolve: Is there something causing you suffering in your life right now? Ask God to use this suffering for a greater good and choose to offer it up as a prayer.

Reach Out: Make a spiritual bouquet (a set of prayers you are committing to pray, such as a certain number of Rosaries or Holy Hours) for others who are ill or elderly, and send them a card to let them know you are thinking about them and praying for them. If you can't think of anyone you know personally, then ask your parish for a list of homebound parishioners.

Pray: Pray every day this week for a greater respect for the dignity of all human life at all stages.

NOTES

NOTES

PART 4
THE COMMON GOOD, PERSONHOOD, SOLIDARITY, SUBSIDIARITY:
THE PRINCIPLES OF THE CHURCH'S SOCIAL DOCTRINE

▸ "A faithful friend is a sturdy shelter: he that has found one has found a treasure."

—Sirach 6:14

▶ Behind DOCAT

Have you ever heard the saying, "The whole is greater than the sum of its parts"? This phrase was coined by the famous Greek philosopher Aristotle in the fourth century. Today the concept is also known by the term "synergy," from the Greek word for "working together." The idea is that in many situations a group is able to accomplish more than the sum of what each part of the group could accomplish on its own. It might be multiple elements coming together to form a compound that has different properties than the two elements do separately (like hydrogen and oxygen forming water) or a group of people accomplishing more together than would be accomplished by each person working on his own.

The Church's social doctrine consists of four main principles, and here also the whole is greater than the sum of its parts. Working together, these four principles accomplish something greater than if each of them were applied separately from the others.

▶ Read DOCAT

Read nos. 84–94.

▶ What Does DOCAT Say?

1. What are the principles of Catholic social teaching?

2. What do we mean by "the common good"?

3. What is the relationship between private property and a democratic economic order?

4. What is the "preferential option for the poor"?

▶ DO reflect

We live in a world with an "us or them" kind of mentality. From sports to politics to entertainment, everything is a competition with clearly defined winners and losers. The Church's social teaching offers a different approach: we are all in this together. The right to private property and the preferential option for the poor are not opposing ideals that we need to find a way to balance. Rather they are two sides of the same coin, and both are vital to the common good.

Everything that we have should be at the service of others. My good depends on the good of my neighbor. Of course, I need to take care of myself—but I also need to keep my focus on the big picture and be concerned about the good of all. It's a simple principle, but because of our fallen human nature, it can be very hard to put into practice.

1. How would you define the common good? Does the common good concern you personally? Why or why not?

2. Do you believe that you need to consider the good of others when you use your own private property? Why or why not?

3. St. Paul said about the Church that "if one member suffers, all suffer together" (1 Corinthians 12:26). Do you think this holds true for humanity as a whole? If so, how does the suffering of others affect you? If not, why not?

▶ What Does the Bible Say?

1. Read Proverbs 11:24–25. According to these verses, what is the result of generosity? What is the result of selfishness?

2. One of the themes of the prophet Isaiah's message is that for our worship to be acceptable to God, we must also love our neighbor. Read Isaiah 58:6-9a. In what ways is God asking us to deny ourselves (fast) in order to honor him? What effect does Isaiah promise for this type of fasting?

3. Chapter 3 of Luke's gospel tells us about the people coming to St. John the Baptist for guidance. Read Luke 3:10–14. What instructions does St. John give the people?

DO Chat

1. What are some ways that our society protects the interests of individuals (private property, for example)? What are some ways that our society promotes the common good? Do you think these two categories are in harmony or in conflict? Why?

2. Do you think that every person has a social obligation to take care of the needs of others? If so, what should this look like? If not, why not?

DO Challenge

Thank: "Every perfect gift is from above" (James 1:17). Everything you have is a gift from God. Start each day this week by thanking God for a new day. Before you go to sleep each night, make a list of what you are thankful for that day.

Give: Take inventory of your personal property: clothes, books, technology, etc. Find something that you are not using productively and give it to someone who has greater need of it than you do.

NOTES

THINK GLOBALLY, ACT LOCALLY

▶ Behind DOCAT

We all know how important it is for us to eat our fruits and vegetables. But some people assert that it's also important that we eat locally grown produce when possible. Eating locally can be healthier for us (higher nutrient content due to ripeness and freshness), healthier for the environment (less need for energy and packaging to ship it long distances), and healthier for the community (supporting local farmers).

This is very similar to the principle of subsidiarity, one of the four principles of Catholic social doctrine. Subsidiarity essentially means keeping things local when possible—making decisions and taking care of problems at the smallest level possible. On the other hand, the social teaching of the Church tells us that we are all part of one, big human family. We are dependent on others and we are responsible for others. This is the principle of solidarity. The beautiful wisdom of these two principles is that we are called to focus on both the local community and the global one. Both are necessary to the good of the individual and to the common good, and we each have responsibilities to both.

▶ Read DOCAT

Read nos. 95–103.

▶ What Does DOCAT Say?

1. What is subsidiarity?
2. What is solidarity?

DO reflect

When they are applied together, the principles of subsidiarity and solidarity mean that we all have responsibilities that belong to us, and that we are responsible for helping others when they need it. It is a balance between fulfilling our own obligations without passing the buck to someone higher up and being willing to take on the needs of someone else as if they were our own.

Human nature tends toward extremes. People sometimes favor one principle to the exclusion of the other: everyone is responsible for himself and owes no one else anything or someone can't take care of himself and so someone else (for example, the government) needs to handle it completely. Both extremes deny the dignity of the human person, but the two principles working together allow each of us to live up to our full potential both by taking on proper responsibility and offering charity.

1. Do you believe that you have a responsibility to participate actively in society? Why or why not?

2. Think about the principle of subsidiarity. What responsibilities can you take care of without passing them on to someone else? On what levels (family, school, community, etc.) can you participate to take care of the responsibilities properly belonging to those groups?

▶ What Does the Bible Say?

1. Pope Leo XIII used the term "friendship" to talk about the same principle we now call solidarity. The Bible has a lot to say on the topic of friendship. Look up the following verses and summarize what it means to be a friend and to show solidarity with others: Proverbs 17:17; Proverbs 27:17; Sirach 6:14–17.

DO Chat

1. What is one way you have seen the principle of subsidiarity applied? What was positive about this approach? What was negative?

2. How does solidarity contribute to a "civilization of love"?

3. Does Jesus's example of solidarity inspire you to act in a particular way? If so, how? If not, why not?

DO Challenge

Remember: Keep in mind the principle of subsidiarity throughout the week, and be mindful of what responsibilities you have. Do your best to fulfill your responsibilities promptly and cheerfully, asking for help if needed but being careful not to shirk your obligations by passing them on to someone else.

Give: Find a local charity to support in some way (volunteering, making a donation, helping to promote their cause, etc.).

Notice: Keep in mind the principle of solidarity throughout the week: look for as many ways as you can find to offer help and support before you are asked.

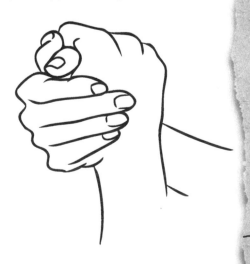

NOTES

Behind DOCAT

"If you don't stand for something, you'll fall for anything." It is a truism that in order to live a meaningful and purpose-driven life, we must live according to some kind of value system. Whether we are motivated by honor, fame, love, money, or anything else, whatever we value most will end up driving our actions and defining our entire lives. Mahatma Gandhi put it this way: "Your values become your destiny."

The Church didn't come up with the principles of its social teaching arbitrarily—they are derived from the natural law written upon our hearts that must be heeded if we desire a *good life*. Her social teaching also flows from the values necessary for a *godly life*. If we truly let these values shape our words and actions, then we will begin to see healing and transformation in all areas of society.

▶ Read DOCAT

Read nos. 104–111.

▶ What Does DOCAT Say?

1. What values are necessary for the successful coexistence of people?

2. What is true freedom?

3. Why is truth important to society?

4. What is justice?

DO reflect

Justice and mercy sometimes appear to be polar opposites. We might think of justice in terms of punishment: if someone breaks the law, then he has to suffer the consequences, and that is justice. On the other hand, someone is considered merciful when she is forgiving or lenient: a merciful judge might give a very light sentence to someone convicted of a crime. The Old Testament seems to emphasize God's justice, dealing out plagues and curses and Jesus's exile to unrepentant sinners. But in the New Testament we see God's mercy very clearly in Jesus's message of love and reconciliation and in his sacrifice on the Cross. This apparent inconsistency even led some people in the second century to start teaching that there were actually two gods: the wrathful god of the Old Testament and the loving god of the New Testament. But God is perfect and infinite—he cannot change, and he cannot contradict himself. Therefore, God isn't merciful part of the time and just the rest of the time. Instead, he is always merciful and always just. When he lets us suffer the consequences of our sins, it is the merciful act of a loving Father showing us that sin won't truly make us happy. When he forgives our sins and fills us with grace, he is justly fulfilling the promises he has made to us.

 Have you ever experienced justice and mercy together from someone (a parent, a teacher, a friend)? How was their justice merciful and their mercy just?

 What does justice without mercy look like? In what ways does this fall short of God's plan for us?

▶ What Does the Bible Say?

1. According to John 8:32, what is the relationship between truth and freedom?

2. It can be easy to confuse "justice" with "revenge." What does Romans 12:19 say about revenge? What do you think this verse can teach us about justice?

3. What does Isaiah 30:18–19 say about the relationship between God's justice and his mercy?

4. Read Micah 6:8 and Zechariah 7:9. What instructions do these prophets give for living a good, godly life?

DO Chat

1. What do you think happens when you have justice without mercy? What about mercy without justice? Have you witnessed any examples of these situations?

2. Do you think we have enough honesty in our society? Why or why not?

DO Challenge

Resolve: Remember the value of freedom this week by consciously choosing the good at every opportunity.

Notice: Be aware of how the truth that you speak and the integrity with which you act makes your relationships with others possible.

Choose: Are you holding onto a grudge or hurt feelings? Choose to forgive the person who wronged you. Ask God for help in forgiving him or her.

NOTES

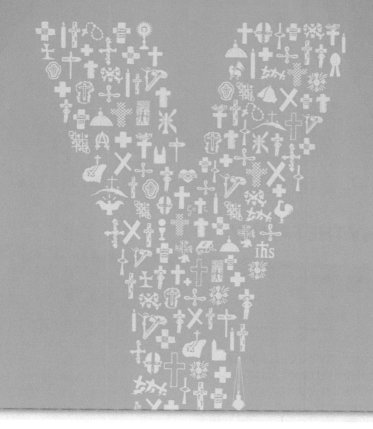

PART 5

THE FOUNDATION OF SOCIETY: THE FAMILY

▶ *"It is not good that the man should be alone."*

—Genesis 2:18

TOPIC 1 | **WHY THE FAMILY?**

▶ Behind DOCAT

What is your earliest memory? Who is the first person you see every day? Who is the last person you talk to before going to bed? With whom do you eat your meals? Who knows you best? To whom do you turn for help? Encouragement? Companionship? Chances are, the answer to at least some of these questions involves your family.

The importance of family goes back to the very beginning. When God created Mankind, he created us for family: he created the first man and the first woman, and he commanded them to be fruitful and multiply. God also uses families to advance his saving plan. The first covenants God made were with families: with Adam and Eve in the Garden of Eden and then with Noah and his family after the flood. In fact, the whole point of a covenant is making two previously unrelated people, or groups, family. In his covenants, God makes us his family. For all these reasons, the family has a very special place in God's plan.

▶ Read DOCAT

Read nos. 112–119.

▶ What Does DOCAT Say?

1. What is the first and most natural community to which we belong?

2. What four things does the family do for society?

▶ DO reflect

The family is where we first learn how to love. Scripture often describes God's love for us in terms of how a parent loves a child—there is no stronger, more fundamental attachment. The family is a miniature civilization of love, and the love we experience in the family we then take and apply to the rest of the world.

At least that's what God intended. There are many challenges facing families in our world, and because of the immeasurable importance of the family, its protection and support are a major priority for the Church. As St. John Paul II said, "As the family goes, so goes the nation, and so goes the whole world in which we live."

1 How have you experienced love in your family? How has this affected your interactions and relationships with people outside your family?

2 What challenges or difficulties has your family faced? Were you able to overcome them? If so, how? If not, what kind of support might have helped?

▶ What Does the Bible Say?

1. Read Genesis 5:1–3. Compare the use of the word "likeness" in verses 1 and 3. What does this tell you about the relationship between God and Adam compared to the relationship between Adam and Seth? What does this say about God's relationship to all of humanity?

2. In Deuteronomy 6, Moses gives Israel the greatest commandment and the most important prayer, called the *Shema* (meaning "hear" in Hebrew). Read Deuteronomy 6:4–9. What does this passage say about the purpose of the family in regard to prayer and instruction? Based on this, what role do you think the family is supposed to play in the life of faith?

DO Chat

1. Do you think that the family has a central role to play in social life? Can any single other community do everything that the family is supposed to do? Why or why not?

2. What are the effects on the human person and on the greater community when the family is not a place of unconditional love?

DO Challenge

Act: Do something this week to show your family how much you appreciate them.

Pray: None of us loves perfectly all the time, and no family is perfect. Take time each day this week to ask God to strengthen your family and to heal any hurts or divisions.

Read: Read one of the papal documents on the family. You can find a list online at http://www.vatican.va/themes/famiglia_test/santopadre_en.htm.

NOTES

TOPIC 2 ────────
CHILDREN AND MARRIAGE

 Behind DOCAT

"First comes love, then comes marriage, then comes a baby in a baby carriage!" For generations children have teased each other over their crushes with variations on this rhyme. Even at a young age it is taken for granted that the logical progression of a romantic relationship is to marriage and then children.

When God created the first man and woman, he told them to "be fruitful and multiply" (Genesis 1:28). The fruitfulness of a husband and wife may be expressed through having biological children, adopting children, fostering children, or mentoring and supporting children in other ways. Marriage is meant to be fruitful because it is, as the *Catechism* says, a "sign and image" of the communion of the Father and the Son in the Holy Spirit in the Trinity (*CCC* 2205). This means that families are by nature intergenerational—family members of all ages make a vital contribution to the life of the family.

▶ **Read DOCAT**

Read nos. 120–129.

▶ **What Does DOCAT Say?**

1. Who has the primary right and duty to raise and educate children?

2. What is marriage?

3. How are family and marriage related?

DO reflect

In his letter to the Ephesians, St. Paul writes that wives should "be subject to [their] husbands, as to the Lord" (Ephesians 5:22). This verse gets a bad rap because it sounds like he is saying that husbands are always in charge and wives don't get to make decisions. But that isn't what St. Paul means at all! The passage begins by saying "Be subject to **one another** out of reverence for Christ" (Ephesians 5:21). So husbands and wives are to be mutually submissive to each other. The husband does have a special position of authority (St. Paul says "the husband is the head of the wife" in verse 23), but this authority requires husbands to "love your wives, as Christ loved the Church and gave himself up for her" (Ephesians 5:25). That's a tall order for husbands, because it means constant self-sacrifice as they put their wives first. In God's plan for marriage, men and women have equal dignity and value, but they have different roles to play. Those roles mirror the relationship between Christ and his Church, and the grace of a holy marriage can work great things not only in the lives of a couple but in the lives of all those around them.

1 Do you believe that men and women are equal in dignity? Do you believe that they have intrinsic differences? Why or why not?

2 Have you ever witnessed a marriage like the kind that St. Paul describes in Ephesians 5:21–33? If so, describe it. If not, what do you think that kind of marriage would look like?

▶ What Does the Bible Say?

1. Look up Genesis 2:21–24. What does this passage say about marriage?

2. What does St. Paul tell us about the duty of children to their parents and parents to their children in Ephesians 6:1–4?

3. Read Psalm 127:3–5 and Proverbs 17:6. What do these verses teach us about the value of children?

DO Chat

1. What does it mean for parents to be the primary educators of their children? What are some different ways that parents can fulfill this responsibility?

2. Do you have any close intergenerational relationships (someone significantly older than you) other than with your parents? What benefits do older relatives bring to family life?

DO Challenge

Pray: Take some time to pray about your vocation—are you called to marriage and parenthood? If you think you might be called to marriage, pray for your future spouse.

NOTES

▶ Behind DOCAT

Nature is full of mutually beneficial, symbiotic relationships, like a clown fish living in an anemone. The clown fish chases away fish that want to feed on the anemone, and the stinging tentacles of the anemone provide protection for the clown fish from predators.

The state and the family also have the potential for a symbiotic relationship, each benefiting the other. The family doesn't exist only for its own sake; every part of society benefits from strong families. For this reason, it's in the best interest of any government to be supportive of families. Of course, the government has to be careful not to violate the principle of subsidiarity by usurping the choices or duties that rightfully belong to the family. But because the family is the foundation of the entire social order, it is only just that the government support and protect the family.

▶ Read DOCAT

Read nos. 130–133.

▶ What Does DOCAT Say?

1. Is it ever right for a government to determine how many children a couple may have?

2. What should be the goal of a government's family policies?

DO reflect

Strong families are in the best interest of the State, but the government cannot tell families to have either more or fewer children. This would violate the dignity of the family and the principle of subsidiarity. The family is for children and children are for the family—therefore to put a limit on the number of children a family may have is to deny the purpose and the dignity of the family. Even if there may be grave reasons for a couple to consider not having another child at a particular time—in which case the couple may have recourse to natural family planning (NFP), a method of avoiding pregnancy that respects the dignity of each spouse and the life-giving nature of marriage—that is a decision that can only be made by that couple. It would contradict the principle of subsidiarity to take that decision away from the family. While it is right and good for the state to make it easier for families to welcome children, human dignity and the dignity of marriage demand that the decision to have children be left to the couple and never coerced.

1. How big is your family? What do you like or dislike about the size of your family?

2. Do you think there is an ideal family size? Why or why not?

3. Why do you think some governments might try to control the size of families? Do you think those reasons are justifiable?

▶ What Does the Bible Say?

1. Read Proverbs 22:6. How does this verse illustrate what the family does for society?

2. Consider what Jesus says about marriage in Mark 10:9. Although Jesus is talking primarily about divorce, how does this verse also shed light on why the government does not have authority to usurp a husband and wife's decisions about children?

DO Chat

1. Do you think governments should play any role in supporting or encouraging the family? If so, in what ways should a government do this? If not, why not?

2. In keeping with the principle of subsidiarity, in what ways can local communities support and encourage families?

DO Challenge

Think: Consider the ways that you interact with society outside of your family. How has family life prepared you for this? Think of an area where you still have something to learn or some improvement to make, and ask your family for help.

Learn: Interview some family members (parents, grandparents, aunts or uncles) to find out how they feel the government succeeds in supporting families and in what ways the government could improve.

NOTES

NOTES

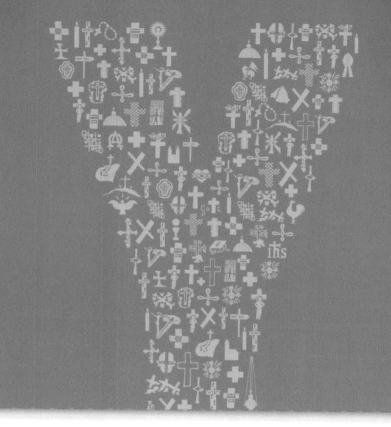

PART 6
OCCUPATION AND VOCATION: HUMAN WORK

▶ "Choose an occupation that you like, and you need not work another day in your life."

—Asian proverb

TOPIC 1 | CO-WORKERS WITH GOD

▶ **Behind DOCAT**

What do you think Jesus did for the thirty years of his life before he started his pubic ministry? The Bible doesn't give us a lot of details. We read about his early years: his birth in Bethlehem, the visits from the shepherds and the magi, and his family's flight to Egypt to escape the murderous King Herod. Then we read about his journey to Jerusalem for the feast of Passover when he was twelve and how Mary and Joseph searched for him for three days before finding him in the Temple. But that's all the Gospels say about the "hidden years" before Jesus started teaching and working miracles.

Tradition fills in some of the gaps. Joseph was a carpenter, so Jesus would have learned that trade from an early age and practiced it as an adult. He spent three years in his public ministry, but he spent ten times that time in quiet family life and diligent work. We're used to paying attention to what Jesus said and did in those last three years of his life, but there is also a very important message in the way he lived for the first thirty years.

▶ **Read DOCAT**

Read nos. 134–138.

▶ **What Does DOCAT Say?**

1. What is the relationship between work and Original Sin?

2. What does Jesus teach us about work?

3. What is the proper place of work in a Christian's priorities?

▶ DO reflect

When God placed Adam in the Garden of Eden, he commanded him to "till it and keep it" (Genesis 2:15). The same Hebrew words are used together again in God's instructions for the priests and Levites serving in the sanctuary of the Tabernacle (see Numbers 3:7–8; 8:26; and 18:5–6). Reading Genesis 2 in light of Numbers shows that mankind's work in the Garden was not just physical labor but a divine work as well—a type of worship. This connection between work and worship is reflected in the language the Church uses to talk about worship. The word "liturgy" comes from two Greek words literally meaning "public work." Liturgy is a special type of work that we offer specifically to God, but all of our work is meant to be directed toward God in some way.

1 In what ways are worship and work similar or connected? In what ways are they different?

2 How can you offer your work to God as a kind of divine service?

▶ What Does the Bible Say?

1. Read Genesis 2:15. What kinds of work do you think would be involved in fulfilling this command? What additional information does Genesis 2:19–20 give about Adam's work in the Garden of Eden?

2. Read Genesis 3:17–19 and Sirach 7:15. The "curse" in Genesis is not an arbitrary punishment for Adam's sin; rather, it expresses the way sin has broken the harmony between mankind and nature that originally existed in God's creation. Does it make a difference in how you view work to see it as an original call from God and fruitless toil as a result of the brokenness caused by sin? How so, or why not?

DO Chat

1. Do you find happiness in any kind of work? If so, what kind? If not, why not? Do you think any kind of work might be able to help make you happy?

2. What do you think about the years Jesus spent working as a carpenter? Is it significant that the God of the universe would spend so many years laboring as an ordinary craftsmen? How so, or why not?

DO Challenge

Thank: Choose to focus on the dignity and importance of your work (whether it's a job outside your home, chores around the house, schoolwork, or something else). Make a resolution to do every task to the best of your ability for the greater glory of God.

Pray: Start every day this week with a prayer asking Jesus and St. Joseph to help you do the work of the day well.

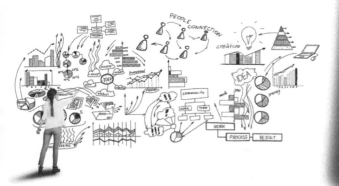

NOTES

WORK FOR MAN, NOT MAN FOR WORK

▶ Behind DOCAT

You are a human being, not a human doing. Work is important, good, and necessary. But, despite the messages of a society obsessed with productivity and achievement, work is not everything. It is not our ultimate purpose, it does not define us, and it should not separate us from our fellow man. Working is part of what we were created to do, but it is not who we were created to be. You might say that God made work for man, not man for work.

Work has an inherent dignity because it is performed by human beings—men and women do not derive their dignity from the work that they do. Society often gets this turned around, but in his great wisdom, God gave us the Sabbath rest in part to protect us from making a false god out of work. And when we remember to honor the dignity of our fellow men, we won't fall into the trap of defining a person by the work he or she does.

▶ Read DOCAT

Read nos. 139–146.

▶ What Does DOCAT Say?

1. What is the purpose of the commandment to rest on the Sabbath?

2. Why is the Church opposed to Marxism? What type of solution does the Church offer instead?

3. What is the objective dimension of work? What is the subjective dimension?

4. What does the Church mean by the "universal destination of material goods"?

DO reflect

The account of God resting on the seventh day of creation can make it seem like God was tired after all the hard work of creation and needed to take a break. Of course God is all-powerful and never needs to rest (see Psalm 121:3– 4). Instead, God rests as a sign of his perfect peace and happiness. He also rests in order to set an example for us. We get tired from our work and we need to take time to recharge, both physically and emotionally. But sometimes we don't notice that we need to take a break—or maybe we feel like we can't afford to take a day off to rest because whatever we are doing is so important. God gives us the command to rest on the Sabbath.

But the Sabbath isn't just about resting from our labors—it is also about worship. God is constantly holding all of creation in existence, and he is actively loving and caring for each of us at every moment. By resting on the Sabbath and giving our full attention to worshipping God, we are reminded that we don't accomplish anything without God.

① Do you make Sunday a day of rest? Why or why not?

② Setting aside the seventh day as a day of rest and worship is also an image of Heaven. What can you do to keep your focus on Heaven as your goal on Sundays?

③ Some work still has to be done on Sundays— some jobs require them to be there on Sundays. If you have work that cannot be avoided on Sunday, what can you do to still keep the Sabbath holy?

▶ What Does the Bible Say?

1. Look up Genesis 2:1–3. Which day is set aside in creation? Why is it set aside?

2. Read Exodus 20:8–11; 23:12; and Deuteronomy 5:12–15. According to these passages, what are the reasons for the Sabbath rest on the seventh day?

DO Chat

1. Do you think that it is possible to achieve a just balance of interests between economic classes, or do you think that a kind of class warfare is inevitable? Why?

2. Do you think that society focuses more on the objective or the subjective dimension of work? Why? Is this positive or negative?

DO Challenge

Decide: Make a decision to set aside next Sunday as a day of rest and worship. Plan to complete all necessary schoolwork, chores, etc., ahead of time so that you do not need to use time on Sunday to finish them.

Meditate: Reflect carefully on the words of Genesis 2:3, "So God blessed the seventh day and hallowed it." Ask God to help you understand what it means for the Sabbath to be holy.

NOTES

TOPIC 3 | **THE RIGHTS OF THE WORKER**

▶ Behind DOCAT

Among the list of human rights are certain rights that relate specifically to work. Because governments have a responsibility to make laws that protect human rights, the state also has an interest in passing laws protecting the rights of workers. As with other rights, the rights of the worker stem from his inherent dignity as a human being. In questions of unemployment, migrant workers, maternity leave, just wage, and all other labor issues, it is important to remember that not only profits and losses are at stake—at the heart of the matter is a human person, beloved by God.

▶ Read DOCAT

Read nos. 147–157.

▶ What Does DOCAT Say?

1. Why do we speak of a "moral right" to work?

2. Why are labor laws necessary? What kind of rights should they protect?

3. What factors should be taken into consideration in determining whether or not a wage is just?

▶ What Does the Bible Say?

1. Look up the following passages: Deuteronomy 24:14–15; Sirach 34:20–22; and Jeremiah 22:13. What does Scripture have to say about the just treatment of workers?

2. Read Isaiah 58:3–7 and James 5:1–6. How does a person's treatment of his workers affect his relationship with God?

DO reflect

In his apostolic exhortation *Evangelii Gaudium*, Pope Francis warns against the dangers of a "throw-away culture" in which people are used as a means for gain and then discarded when they are no longer useful or convenient. This kind of abuse of our fellow man isn't limited to big businesses and wealthy corporations. It is easy for anyone to fall into this mentality in a society driven by consumerism. Greed leads people to try to acquire as much as they can, no matter who they have to step on in the process. On the other hand, it takes self-control and humility to recognize that the rights and dignity of others are more important than our own desires.

1. Do you have any relationships in your life where you might be using someone as a means to an end? If so, what can you do to fix that relationship? If not, how can you guard against falling into that trap?

2. Are you ever in a position of authority over someone else (such as babysitting, a supervisory position at your job, leading a group project, etc.)? How can you treat the people around you with the respect that they deserve?

DO Chat

1. Which workers' rights do you think are well-protected? Which ones need greater protection?

2. Do you think anything can be done to foster a sense of solidarity between employers and employees? If so, what? If not, is there any solution for conflicts of interest between the two groups?

3. What can be done to improve the balance between work and family life? Think about various levels of solutions: government, industry, community, individual, etc.

DO Challenge

Study: Carefully read and review what DOCAT and the Church documents have to say about the rights of workers so that you can explain not only what the Church teaches but also why.

NOTES

NOTES

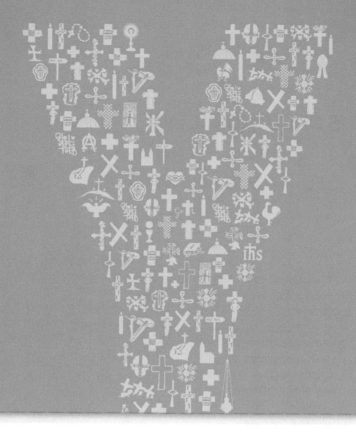

PART 7

WELFARE AND JUSTICE FOR ALL: ECONOMIC LIFE

▶ "In the economic and social realms, too, the dignity and complete vocation of the human person and the welfare of society as a whole are to be respected and promoted. for man is the source, the center, and the purpose of all economic and social life."

—Vatican Council II, Gaudium et Spes, 63

▶ Behind DOCAT

Economic activity is as old as civilization. Every person has material needs such as food, shelter, and clothing. Very few people are in a position to provide for each of these needs on their own, so the majority of us rely on some kind of economic system to obtain what we need. Whether we pay for goods with money or barter our own products or services in exchange for what we need, we are one piece of a vast economic system that, ideally, allows individuals to offer something that they have in order to obtain everything else that they need.

Over the course of human history, economic life has taken many forms. Even today there are many different types of economies around the world. The Church concerns herself with economic life because an economy is not just about goods and services—it is about the human person.

▶ Read DOCAT

Read nos. 158–170.

▶ What Does DOCAT Say?

1. What is the goal of economic activity?

2. What is a market economy? What is necessary for this type of economy to be ethically acceptable?

3. What do we mean by "development"?

4. What kind of economic activity does the Church support?

5. What kind of poverty is always bad? What kind of poverty can lead to good?

▶ DO reflect

Some people believe that real faith in God will be rewarded with material prosperity—that the signs of God's favor are health and wealth. This so-called "Prosperity Gospel" focuses on the treasures of this world, but the Church reminds us of Jesus's call to lay aside anxiety about this world and seek first God and his Kingdom. While money and good health are certainly good things, they are not the highest good.

Men and women with a vocation to religious life live out this call in a beautiful, radical way when they take their vow of poverty. This vow doesn't mean that they choose to live below the poverty line, but it does mean that the members of the order renounce private ownership of possessions. They live a life modeled on Acts 2:44: "And all who believed were together and had all things in common." In doing so they offer an example of what it looks like to seek God's Kingdom first and store up treasures in Heaven. Giving up all private property isn't practical for most laypeople. But we are all called to store up our treasure in Heaven rather than here on earth, and being careful not to be overly attached to material goods is an important start.

1. What distracts you from seeking God and his Kingdom? Why?

2. What do you think is a healthy attachment to possessions? How would you describe your attachment to your own possessions?

3. What is one thing you can do to put God and his Kingdom first in your life?

▶ What Does the Bible Say?

1. Read the Parable of the Talents in Matthew 25:14–30. What does this parable teach us about what we are supposed to do with the resources made available to us?

2. Look up the Parable of the Rich Fool in Luke 12:16–21. What does this story say about looking for security and fulfillment in material possessions? According to Luke 12:32–34, what should we focus on instead?

3. What does Jesus say about anxiety in Matthew 6:25–34? What does St. Paul say about anxiety in Philippians 4:6–7? What do you think is the difference between being anxious about the future and planning ahead?

DO Chat

1. How do economics and ethics fit together? Why is something that is unethical also bad economics? Why is something that is uneconomical also unethical?

2. How would you define "consumerism"? Do you agree that, in a certain sense, consumerism makes people even poorer? Why or why not?

3. What does it mean to store up treasures in Heaven? How is that compatible or incompatible with earthly treasure?

DO Challenge

Pray: Pray the Our Father every day this week, focusing on the words "Give us this day our daily bread." Remember to ask God for everything that you need and to thank him for all the ways he provides for you.

Memorize: Memorize Philippians 4:6.

Think: Make a list of your top ten "treasures"—whatever is most important to you in life (things, people, ideas, etc.). Which of these are earthly treasures and which are heavenly treasures?

NOTES

TOPIC 2 —————
MORE THAN NUMBERS

▶ Behind DOCAT

Mark's Gospel tells the story of a poor widow bringing her offering to the Temple. Although she only contributed two small coins, Jesus said that this woman gave more than all the rich people bringing large sums of money because she gave all that she had (*cf.* Mark 12:41–44). The spirit of her gift was more important than the amount. In the same way, economic systems must be judged by their spirit—how they view the human person—and not just by their promise of success.

It's easy to think about economics in terms of numbers: profit and loss, production capacity, supply and demand, etc. But an economic system that puts anything ahead of the dignity of the human person is fundamentally unethical. For this reason economics can't be approached as just a numbers game.

▶ Read DOCAT

Read nos. 171–181.

▶ What Does DOCAT Say?

1. What type of capitalism is compatible with human dignity? What type of capitalism is not?

2. What is a "free market"?

3. What type of competition is good? What type of competition is a sin against love of neighbor?

DO reflect

"Blessed are you poor, for yours is the kingdom of God.... But woe to you that are rich, for you have received your consolation" (Luke 6:20b, 24). With a message like this, it would be easy to conclude that wealth is objectively evil. In another place Jesus even says that "it is easier for a camel to go through the eye of a needle than for a rich man to enter the kingdom of God" (Mark 10:25). But money isn't the problem—having the wrong priorities is. Profit, private property, competition—these things are not inherently bad. But when we prioritize them over love of God and neighbor, then we are in serious trouble. Money by itself won't keep us from eternal life but greed and selfishness will. Practicing moderation, love of neighbor, and justice will help us keep our priorities straight when it comes to money.

 1 Do you ever feel tempted by greed and selfishness? Do you think these temptations are at all related to how much you possess? Why or why not?

2 How might practicing moderation help protect us from excessive love of money?

▶ What Does the Bible Say?

1. Read Matthew 6:24. What do you think it means to serve mammon (riches)? Why isn't this compatible with serving God?

2. What does Jesus say about himself and his Kingdom in John 18:36? What does this mean for us if we are seeking his Kingdom?

DO Chat

1. What do you think is the relationship between material progress and the Kingdom of God? Why?

2. Although there is no such thing as a "Christian economic model" (no. 172), what factors would make certain economic models more or less compatible with the message of the Gospel?

3. What do you think justice and love of neighbor look like practically when lived out in the economic life? How are these factors both ethical and good for economics?

DO Challenge

Notice: Go out of your way to honor the dignity of other people in your economic activity this week: ask your cashier how her day is going, smile at and thank your barista, compliment your waiter on something, etc.

NOTES

▶ Behind DOCAT

In 1 Timothy 6:10, St. Paul warns his young disciple Timothy that "the love of money is the root of all evils." Greed is a serious problem—even causing some to turn their backs on the faith, according to St. Paul—so it isn't surprising that in an attempt to avoid greed it is easy to err in the opposite direction and start thinking of money itself as evil. The Church's social teaching helps us keep our perspective. Money is neither moral nor immoral; what we choose to do with it (and what we let money do to us) is where the potential for good and evil lies.

▶ Read DOCAT

Read nos. 182–194.

▶ What Does DOCAT Say?

1. What is the main task of the state in the economic life?

2. What does justice in business look like?

3. What do people need besides simple economic growth?

DO reflect

Acts 16:11–15 offers an example of the good that someone can do with their business. When Sts. Paul, Silas, Timothy, and Luke arrived in Philippi, they met a businesswoman named Lydia. Lydia was a "seller of purple goods" (Acts 16:14), a very profitable business in the ancient world. When Lydia heard the Gospel, she and her entire household were immediately baptized. Her prosperous situation and respected standing in the community allowed her to be a great help to St. Paul and his companions. They stayed in Lydia's home during their time in Philippi, and Lydia and the other Philippian believers continued to send monetary support to St. Paul after he continued on his missionary journey. The Christians in Philippi likely met for prayer and worship in her home, making her house the first Christian church in Europe. Lydia put her economic success at the service of Christ and his Church, and we are invited to do the same.

1 Do you have a job? Do you do any volunteer work? How do these endeavors help you to become a better Christian?

2 Lydia's success in business gave her an opportunity to help spread the Gospel. What can you do—with your money, time, relationships, etc.—to help spread the Gospel?

▶ What Does the Bible Say?

1. What does Proverbs 16:8 say about priorities within business?

2. Read Psalm 112:5–6. What reward is promised for the one who deals justly and generously with others?

DO Chat

1. What are some pros and cons of a government completely controlling the economy? What are some pros and cons of an economy completely independent of the government?

2. Why do you think Catholic social doctrine outlines a middle ground where the government has roles and responsibilities in the economy but must not overstep its bounds?

3. What are the values and characteristics of a good business? Do you know of any businesses that fit this description?

DO Challenge

Read: Read the account of Lydia's conversion in Acts 16:11–15.

Give: Contribute something to the offertory the next time you go to Mass.

NOTES

NOTES

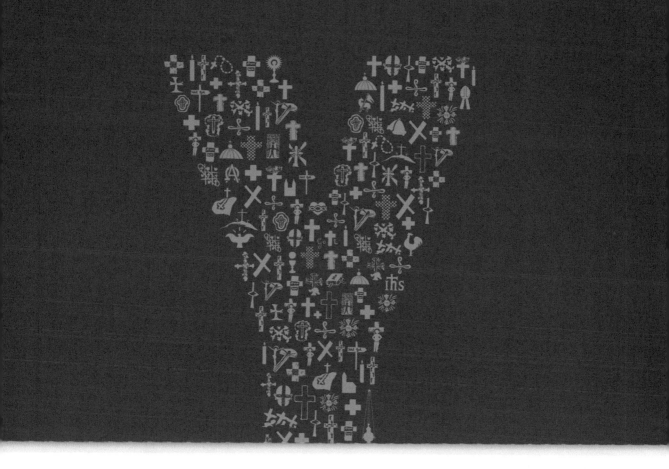

PART 8

POWER AND MORALITY: THE POLITICAL COMMUNITY

▶ "It is evident that a city
is a natural production
and that man is naturally
a political animal."

—Aristotle, Politics

▶ **Behind DOCAT**

If human persons are inherently social—created for community—then there must be some sort of system to organize those living together and interacting within that community. The responsibility for facilitating the peaceful and just coexistence of large groups of people falls to the state. It is both a right and a responsibility of the human person to contribute to the ordering of public life and participate in politics, which are meant to be at the service of the individual and civil society.

▶ **Read DOCAT**

Read nos. 195–203.

▶ **What Does DOCAT Say?**

1. What does Aristotle mean by saying that man is a "political animal"?

2. Why is the state necessary?

3. What is the "third sector"?

4. On what fundamental values do modern democracies rely?

▸ DO reflect

God is the source of all legitimate authority. This doesn't mean that God necessarily approves of every way that authority is used, but it does mean that we owe obedience to people in authority over us as a matter of justice. Part of being a faithful follower of Christ is being a good citizen: obeying laws, contributing to the good of the community, and participating in the political process. This participation is both a right and a duty. It can be tempting to think that one voice won't make a difference in a heated political debate or that one vote won't change the outcome of an election. But the Body of Christ needs all her members working to shape public life for the good of all. We do a disservice both to ourselves and to society if we sit back and fail to do our part.

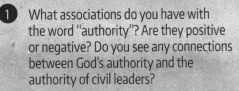

1 What associations do you have with the word "authority"? Are they positive or negative? Do you see any connections between God's authority and the authority of civil leaders?

2 How important to you is your right to participate in the political process? Why?

3 Do you believe that it's important for each person to participate in the political process? Why or why not?

Picture Credit: St. Paul preaching in Athens / © Restored Tradition Art

▶ What Does the Bible Say?

1. What does St. Paul teach about authority in Romans 13:1–7? How does this affect our relationship to the State?

2. Read Wisdom of Solomon 6:1–5. What responsibilities do rulers and governmental leaders have?

3. Psalm 72 is a prayer written by King Solomon for the coronation of his son, Rehoboam. What does this psalm tell us about how a king of God's people was expected to govern? In what ways, if any, can this psalm apply to our expectations of governments today?

DO Chat

1. Where should politics be in a Christian's priorities? How important do you think this ordering of priorities is? Why?

2. How necessary do you think the third sector is? Could government fulfill the same role? Why or why not?

3. In what ways, if any, are the theological common good and the political common good related? What happens if a government tries to define a political common good that is in direct opposition to the theological common good?

DO Challenge

Read: Read paragraphs 1905–1912 in the *Catechism of the Catholic Church* on the common good.

Memorize: Memorize one verse from Psalm 72.

NOTES

GREAT SERVANTS

▶ Behind DOCAT

One of the titles used by popes since the sixth century is "Servant of the Servants of God." Although the pope is a head of state and a spiritual father to millions, his job description is one of service because he leads in imitation of Christ.

It is easy to see how leadership is supposed to be a service to others in the Church, but this is true of political leadership as well. Political leaders should be servants of the people and the common good, not seeking their own gain. A spirit of humility and service in leadership is foundational to shaping civil society into something better.

▶ Read DOCAT

Read nos. 204–213.

▶ What Does DOCAT Say?

1. How has Christianity led to modern democracy?

2. According to Christianity, what is the ultimate binding authority?

3. What standard for leadership did Jesus introduce?

4. What does it mean for all public office to be service?

▶ What Does the Bible Say?

1. Read Jesus's conversation with Pilate in John 18:33-38. What kind of a king is Jesus? What does he say about his Kingdom?

2. Read Jesus's words in Matthew 22:21. What do we owe to the government? What do we owe to God?

DO reflect

Theologians have called the Cross the throne of Christ's love. This is not a comfortable image. The cross was a torturous method of execution, and although it has become for Christians the sign of our salvation, it is still a sign of suffering and death. But it was on the Cross that Jesus fulfilled the will of the Father and achieved victory over sin and death, and so the Cross is also a sign of Christ's sovereignty and triumph. If we are to reign with Christ as promised (cf. 2 Timothy 2:12), it means we must follow Christ's example to lead through service, empty ourselves, and embrace the Cross.

1. Do you think the Cross makes sense as a throne? Why or why not?

2. To the world, the Cross looked like a total defeat. Have you ever experienced something that appeared to be a loss but which God turned into a victory?

3. Jesus didn't skip the suffering of the Cross to get to the glory of the Resurrection. What difficulties and challenges is God calling you to embrace in order to do his will?

Picture Credit: Christ washing the feet of St. Peter / © Restored Tradition Art

DO Chat

1. In what ways was Jesus like a political leader? In what ways was he different from a typical political leader? Are there any dangers in overemphasizing a potential political aspect of Jesus's message?

2. Do you think that democracy has a better framework for the fulfillment of the human person than other types of government? Why or why not? What role should government play in the fulfillment of the human person?

3. Do you know anyone who leads or governs by service? If so, what does that kind of leadership look like? How would you exercise your authority as a servant-leader?

4. How important do you think freedom of information is to participation in the political process? Why?

DO Challenge

Pray: Pick two elected officials to pray for by name every day this week, that God would guide them in a leadership of service pleasing to him.

Memorize: Memorize Matthew 20:28.

NOTES

▶ Behind DOCAT

Freedom of religion is one of the basic rights to which every person is entitled. This means that a government cannot rightfully force any religious belief or observance upon a person, and it also means that a government cannot justly prevent a person from worshipping and living according to his or her faith. The separation of church and state was originally intended to protect religions from the government's interference. In the minds of many people, however, freedom of religion has been replaced by freedom from religion, and in many countries we see increasing hostility toward any public practice or expression of religion. Christians must continue to take part in politics in an authentically Christian way, not just to guarantee the protection of the rights of all but also to demonstrate that one can boldly live a life of faith without impinging on the rights or beliefs of anyone else.

▶ Read DOCAT

Read nos. 214–228.

▶ What Does DOCAT Say?

1. What does laicism/secularism mean, and why is the Church critical of it?

2. What is the central theme of Christian political ethics?

3. What is natural law?

4. What is included in religious freedom?

5. What should be the purpose of punishment for breaking the law?

DO reflect

In his letter to the Christians in Philippi, St. Paul reminds the faithful that we are first and foremost citizens of Heaven (*cf.* Philippians 3:20). Our first allegiance is to God and after him, to earthly authorities. In most cases these loyalties should not be in conflict; a just government does not make laws that are contrary to the natural law or the common good. However, in some cases we may be forced to choose between obedience to God and obedience to human laws.

This makes the moral duty of the Christian to participate in social life even more important. It doesn't look very convincing to refuse to participate in shaping public policy and then complain about the result. We should be working and praying for a government that follows the natural law and serves the common good. No earthly government will be perfect, so this will require patience and trust in God. Together we *can* shape a better earthly society in imitation of our heavenly home.

 1 Do you think it is okay to claim "conscientious objection" any time you don't agree with a law? Why or why not?

2 What does it mean to be a citizen of Heaven? What does it mean to be a citizen of your nation?

▶ What Does the Bible Say?

1. Read 1 Peter 2:13–17. How does St. Peter instruct Christians to live in relation to a secular government?

2. Consider the story of Daniel in the lions' den in Daniel 6:10–23. How does Daniel act when confronted with an unjust law that contradicts God's commandments? What effect do Daniel's actions have on the king?

DO Chat

1. People often cite the separation of church and state as a reason for not allowing religious views to inform political choices. Do you think this is a right understanding of the separation between church and state? Why or why not?

2. What is the role of an individual's conscience in regards to the authority of the state? What conditions must be met in order to justify rejecting the state's authority in a matter of conscience?

3. How important is religious freedom? To what extent should the state protect it? What can we do to promote religious freedom?

DO Challenge

Thank: The next time you go to Mass, take time to thank God for the freedom to worship him. Let your intention for that Mass be the protection of religious freedom all over the world.

Read: Read paragraphs 1897–1927 in the *Catechism of the Catholic Church* on participation in civil society.

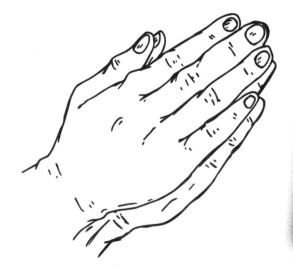

NOTES

NOTES

PART 9

ONE WORLD, ONE HUMANITY: THE INTERNATIONAL COMMUNITY

▸ "The world has a lively feeling of unity and of compelling solidarity of mutual independence."

——Vatican Council II, Gaudium et Spes, 4

▶ Behind DOCAT

As technology allowed for faster, more comprehensive communication, people began using the term "global village" to describe the human community spread across the earth. The vast distances separating groups of people have shrunk due to instantaneous and ubiquitous communication, and the many cultural and linguistic divides have been largely overcome by the massive amounts of information available to anyone who is interested. The metaphor of the village for the global community emphasizes that we are all in this together. We are neighbors separated by oceans, but we are neighbors nonetheless.

▶ Read DOCAT

Read nos. 229–237.

▶ What Does DOCAT Say?

1. What is globalization?

2. What are some of the potential problems related to globalization?

3. What differences are good and acceptable in the human family? What must we not allow to be different between different groups of people?

▶ DO reflect

Genesis 11:1–9 tells the story of the Tower of Babel. After the flood, one group of people tried to assert their own power and independence from God by building a massive tower "with its top in the heavens" (Genesis 11:4). To prevent them from going any further in their prideful revolt, God confused their language; if they couldn't understand one another then they would no longer be able to collaborate in rebellion.

Over two thousand years later, a city full of Jewish pilgrims from various nations and ethnicities heard the gospel message miraculously preached to them, each in his native language (cf. Acts 2:1-12). The coming of the Holy Spirit upon the Apostles at Pentecost healed the wound of division resulting from the sin at Babel. From that point on, the beautiful diversity of the human family is brought into a rich unity of life in the Holy Spirit.

1 Think of a time you had difficulty communicating with someone else. What got in the way of understanding each other? How did you resolve it?

2 Have you ever experienced the Mass in another language? If so, what was the experience like? If not, do you think it would be a valuable experience? Why or why not?

▶ What Does the Bible Say?

1. Read Genesis 3:20. Why does Adam call his wife "Eve"? If Adam and Eve are the first parents of the whole human race, what does this indicate about your relationship with every other person?

2. Genesis 10 is referred to as the "Table of the Nations" because it lists the nations of the ancient Near East world. Read Genesis 10:1 and 10:32. What do the genealogies contained in this chapter indicate about the origins of the various nations?

DO Chat

1. Describe an experience you've had of another culture (for example, studying a language, eating new food, traveling to a different country, etc.). In what ways did this experience impact you?

2. Do you find it easy or difficult to think of the whole human race as one family? Why or why not?

DO Challenge

Learn: Learn to pray the Sign of the Cross in another language.

Read: Read the *Catechism of the Catholic Church* on Liturgy and Culture in paragraphs 1204–1205.

NOTES

TOPIC 2
GLOBAL SOLIDARITY

▶ ### Behind DOCAT

When the Bible tells us to love our neighbor as ourselves, it isn't talking about an abstract or an emotional kind of love—it's talking about action. Part of belonging to the human family is taking care of our brothers and sisters. The needs that we have and the rights that belong to us are universal—if it's true for me then it's true for someone on the other side of the world. Both individuals and nations have the responsibility to care for the needs and advocate for the rights of others, whether they are in our own community or halfway around the world.

▶ ### Read DOCAT

Read nos. 238–247.

▶ ### What Does DOCAT Say?

1. Why does the Church express a "preferential option for the poor"?

2. What is the difference between negative duties and positive duties? What is one example of each?

3. What is self-interest "correctly understood"?

▶ ### What Does the Bible Say?

1. Read the Parable of the Good Samaritan in Luke 10:25–37. In Jesus's time, the Jews and Samaritans wanted absolutely nothing to do with each other—in fact, they had been bitter enemies for over 700 years. With this in mind, what lessons regarding global solidarity can we learn from this parable?

2. Look up Acts 10:34–35 and Romans 10:18. What do these passages say about God's partiality?

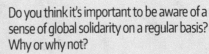

DO reflect

Major tragedies often inspire widespread exhibitions of global solidarity. After a terrorist attack or a huge natural disaster, people all over the world respond with expressions of support and unity. These displays of solidarity are good and beautiful, but we are called to something even greater. The Church reminds us to cultivate this sense of universal brotherhood not only in the face of disaster but always. St. Paul urged the church in Galatia not to "grow weary in well-doing" but to take every opportunity to "do good to all men" (Galatians 6:9–10). The same admonition holds true for us today: solidarity with our brothers and sisters around the world should be a daily consideration. Let's not wait for some catastrophe to remind us of our fellowship with the rest of the world.

1 Why do you think tragic events often renew a sense of global solidarity?

2 Have you ever felt a close connection to someone you've never met? If so, what sparked this connection? If not, what kinds of things do you think could unite you to people you don't know?

3 Do you think it's important to be aware of a sense of global solidarity on a regular basis? Why or why not?

DO Chat

1. Do you think that one group of people can claim certain rights while also denying those rights to other groups of people? Why or why not?

2. In what ways is it in the self-interest of a wealthy nation to help poorer nations? Do you think there are any areas of global relief that would only benefit the recipient and not the giver?

3. In what ways is it in your own self-interest to help others who are in need? In your own community? In other countries?

DO Challenge

Give: Pick an international aid organization and donate something to it (a monetary donation, free publicity by telling others about it, etc.).

Read and Pray: Choose a news source and read about current international events. Pick one news story and pray for the people involved.

▶ **Behind DOCAT**

"The Church is the place where humanity must rediscover its unity and salvation" *(CCC* 845). Globalization brings with it a variety of challenges. Not all players on the global stage have equal roles. There are stronger nations and weaker nations, wealthy states and poor states, war-torn countries and countries experiencing a period of peace. These differences in situation often lead to inequality and injustice.

The Catholic Church is in a unique position to speak to these challenges. On a secular level, the Holy See is an independent city-state and can participate in the international community on the level of other nations. On a spiritual level, the fact that the Church is catholic (universal) means that it is meant for and concerned about every single person. The Second Vatican Council stated that in some sense all people are related to the Church because all people are "called by God's grace to salvation" (*Lumen Gentium,* 13). Whatever difficulties and questions arise with globalization, the Church offers the answer: Jesus and his love for us.

▶ **Read DOCAT**

Read nos. 248–255.

▶ **What Does DOCAT Say?**

1. What are the four key points of Catholic social teaching relating to migrants?

2. What is fair trade?

DO reflect

The Old Testament tells several stories of people welcoming strangers into their lives who later turn out to be angels. Abraham plays host to three unknown travelers who announce the coming birth of Isaac (*cf.* Genesis 18:1–21). Lot welcomes two strangers, and he and his daughters are saved from the destruction of Sodom (*cf.* Genesis 19). Gideon receives a visitor who then helps him deliver Israel from the oppression of its enemies (*cf.* Judges 6–7). And Tobias hires a traveling companion who not only accompanies him on his journey but leads him to his future wife (*cf.* Tobit 5–9). In each of these stories, the virtue of hospitality is rewarded with great blessing. The Letter to the Hebrews urges Christians to imitate these Old Testament figures when it says, "Do not neglect to show hospitality to strangers, for thereby some have entertained angels unawares" (Hebrews 13:2). Whether we are welcoming family, friends, or strangers from near or far, when we show hospitality we are blessing others and honoring God—and we are likely being blessed as well.

① When have you been welcomed by others? What was it like to receive their hospitality?

② What opportunities do you have to show hospitality?

③ Pick one of the stories above and read it. How did that person receive more than he gave when welcoming a stranger? Have you ever felt like you received more than you gave by offering someone hospitality?

▶ What Does the Bible Say?

1. Read Isaiah 49:6. What kind of mission does God have in mind for the prophet Isaiah? Do you think that as a Christian today you have any participation in this same mission? If so, how? If not, why not?

2. Look up Exodus 23:9; Leviticus 19:33–34, and Deuteronomy 10:17–19. What do these passages say about how Israel was supposed to treat immigrants ("sojourners" in the RSV)? What reason does God give for expecting this kind of treatment?

DO Chat

1. Have you ever moved? What was positive about the experience? What was challenging? If you haven't moved, what is positive or negative about having stayed in the same place your whole life?

2. Do you consider whether or not something is "fair trade" when you are making purchases? Do you think this is an important consideration? Why or why not?

DO Challenge

Pray: When you get dressed in the morning, check the tag on each article of clothing to see where it was made. Pray for each of those countries that day.

Learn: Interview your parents, grandparents, or other relatives to learn as much as you can about your genealogy. When did your ancestors come to this country? Where did they come from?

NOTES

NOTES

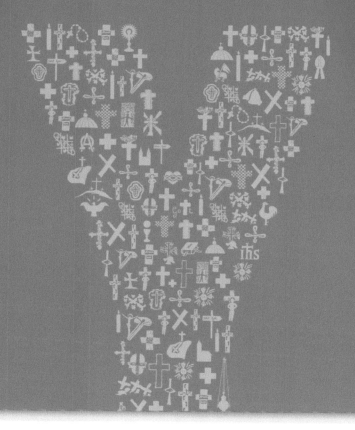

PART 10
SAFEGUARDING CREATION: THE ENVIRONMENT

▶ "God himself is the Creator of the world, and creation is not yet finished. … Thus human work [is] now seen as a special form of human resemblance to God, as a way in which man can and may share in God's activity as creator of the world."

—Pope Benedict XVI, Address, September 12, 2008

TOPIC 1 | STEWARDS OF CREATION

▶ Behind DOCAT

People with a great deal of authority often have a steward to assist them. The Old Testament kings of Judah had stewards to take care of their affairs while they were away from Jerusalem. Jesus told several parables involving masters leaving stewards in charge of their affairs and other servants. And God did the same thing with creation: he set mankind as stewards over creation, to care for the animals and the environment, and to use the resources of the world wisely. Man and woman are at the center of creation, but this place of privilege comes with a great responsibility as well.

▶ Read DOCAT

Read nos. 256–259.

▶ What Does DOCAT Say?

1. Does taking care of creation mean preserving all of nature without change? Why or why not?

2. According to the Church, which people are responsible for taking care of the environment?

▶ What Does the Bible Say?

1. To whom does the world belong, according to Psalm 24:1?

2. What does Sirach 17:1–4 say about God, mankind, and the rest of creation?

▶ DO reflect

The Jews thought of the Temple as a microcosm of creation—the whole world in miniature. And so when Solomon built the Temple in Jerusalem, he had it filled with imagery from nature: a huge bronze basin to call to mind the sea, the great menorah shaped like a tree, golden trees and flowers set with precious stones on the walls, etc. The Temple was the special dwelling place of God with his people, a place of worship and divine encounter. It was designed to call to mind the Garden of Eden, the first place of divine encounter in creation. This imagery in the Temple also indicated that all of creation was originally meant to be a kind of temple—to draw our attention to God and to facilitate an encounter with him. God created and filled the earth and declared it good. Creation is his first gift to us, and he continues to speak to us through it.

1 If all of creation is a type of temple, then what does that say about your role in caring for creation?

2 In what ways do you experience God in nature?

DO Chat

1. What is the relationship between human dignity and environmentalism?

2. Do you think faith in God requires us to care for the environment? If so, why, and in what ways? If not, why not?

3. How would you respond to someone who says that it is wrong for humans to have any impact on the environment?

DO Challenge

Notice: Pay attention to the things you throw away. Find a way to reuse or repurpose some of the items that you would normally throw away.

Choose: Be mindful of the food you eat this week and choose not to waste any of it. Try not to take more than you will eat, and save leftovers to eat later rather than throwing them away.

NOTES

▶ Behind DOCAT

Chances are you at least occasionally borrow something from someone else—a library book, a friend's phone when your battery dies, your sister's sweater, your brother's bike. When you're using something that belongs to someone else, you have a particular responsibility to take care of it and not return it damaged.

This is what it means to be a steward—you take care of something that really belongs to someone else. That's why the Church uses the language of stewardship when it talks about the environment—God has entrusted creation to us, but it doesn't really belong to us. Creation belongs to God, and he intends it for each one of us, from Adam and Eve down to the last person born before the end of the world. We don't just care for our little corner of the environment for its own sake or for ours. We care for it because it is part of the whole, and we're going to have to account to its Creator for its condition when we're done with it.

▶ Read DOCAT

Read nos. 260–262.

▶ What Does DOCAT Say?

1. What are the three main ideas of Catholic environmental ethics?

DO reflect

Near the end of the Book of Revelation, John has a vision of a new heaven and earth: "Then I saw a new heaven and a new earth; for the first heaven and the first earth had passed away....And he who sat upon the throne said, 'Behold, I make all things new'" (Revelation 21:1, 5). God's plan for you is to renew and transform you in his love, and this is God's plan for the rest of the cosmos as well. The *Catechism of the Catholic Church* says that mankind and the material world are both destined to be perfected in God's glory (*cf. CCC* 1046–47). Just as you have an immeasurable and inalienable dignity as a person created in God's image and likeness, so too does creation have inherent dignity and worth because it is from God and destined to be transformed in God. Our stewardship of creation is very much a labor of the present, but it is also a labor directed toward eternity.

 1 Does thinking about the common destiny of mankind and the material world make a difference in how you think about creation and your responsibility as a steward? Why or why not?

2 What can you do to demonstrate a respect for the inherent worth of God's creation?

▶ What Does the Bible Say?

1. What does Psalm 147:7–9, 15–18 say about God's ongoing relationship with his creation?

2. Read Romans 8:18–25. What connection does St. Paul draw between the future of the created world and the salvation of mankind?

3. Look up Ephesians 1:10 and Colossians 1:20. Based on these verses, what spiritual significance does creation have in relation to Christ?

DO Chat

1. What impact does a lifestyle of consumerism have on the environment? What are some steps we can take to shape our lifestyle such that it has a positive effect and not a negative effect on the environment?

2. What goods of creation have been entrusted to you? What do you think it means to use these goods as a steward rather than as an owner, recognizing that they are ordered first to the common good?

DO Challenge

Read: Read Revelation 21.

Notice and Pray: Choose one resource—water, food, electricity, etc.—about which to be especially mindful in your stewardship this week. Whenever you make use of this resource during the week, say a quick prayer for all those around the world who do not have sufficient access to this resource.

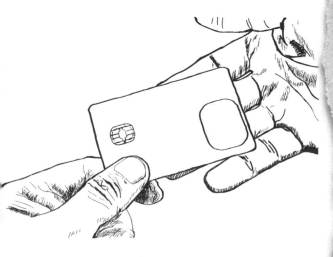

NOTES

TOPIC 3 | **WASTE NOT, WANT NOT**

▶ Behind DOCAT

When we're deciding how to best care for the environment we need to take into consideration not only the present but also the future. Creation is destined for the common good of all humanity, so wasting the goods of creation is actually stealing something from future generations (cf. *CCC* 2415, 2456).

We owe it to God and to future generations to care for the earth and its resources in a way that bears in mind not just our own needs but also the common good. If we use creation mindfully and responsibly then we will have what we need without causing a deficit for other people.

▶ Read DOCAT

Read nos. 263–269.

▶ What Does DOCAT Say?

1. What is the principle of sustainability?
2. What is the ultimate reason behind being concerned about the environment?
3. How is solidarity necessary for sustainability?
4. How is subsidiarity necessary for sustainability?

▶ What Does the Bible Say?

1. Read about the command to observe the Sabbath year in Leviticus 25:1–5. What is the theological importance of this practice for Israel? What is the practical importance? Is there any connection between the two?

DO reflect

Why should you care about sustainability? Sure, it's clearly a good principle, but are your actions really important? It can be so difficult to feel like we are making a difference when we try to measure our individual efforts against a global problem. Aside from the fact that global problems are often solved by the accumulation of individual efforts (in keeping with the conventional wisdom that if you're not part of the solution then you're part of the problem), being a good steward of creation helps you to grow in virtue. In particular, using the earth's resources responsibly is one aspect of the virtue of temperance or moderation. The *Catechism of the Catholic Church* says that temperance "provides balance in the use of created goods" (*CCC* 1809). So when you act as a responsible steward of creation, you are growing in holiness.

 Do you ever find it challenging to be balanced in your use of created goods? If so, what goods (or resources) in particular challenge your temperance? If not, why do you think this comes easily to you?

2 All of the virtues are connected. In what ways might practicing responsible stewardship help you grow in the other cardinal (meaning "pivotal") virtues: prudence (recognizing the good and right way to achieve it), justice (giving both God and neighbor what is due to them), and fortitude (faithfully and firmly pursuing the good)?

DO Chat

1. In what ways do you see resources being used in an unsustainable way? In what ways do you notice resources being used in a moderate and responsible way?

2. Do you think that focusing on sustainability as an ideology can get in the way of making actual progress toward sustainability? Why or why not?

3. What are some helpful steps that can be taken toward sustainability on a local level, even if they fall short of achieving the ideal? On the global level?

DO Challenge

Choose: Identify one resource you use and try to use it more responsibly this week—don't let the water run while you brush your teeth, carpool to school or work instead of driving yourself, walk somewhere instead of driving, etc.

Thank: Write a thank you note or make a donation to a charity that helps make resources more available to people who need them.

NOTES

NOTES

PART 11

LIVING IN FREEDOM FROM VIOLENCE: PEACE

▶ *"Peace I leave with you; my peace I give to you; not as the world gives do I give to you."*

—John 14:27

TOPIC 1 | SHALOM—GOD'S OWN PEACE

▶ Behind DOCAT

"Know Jesus, know peace. No Jesus, no peace." The saying makes for a clever bumper sticker because behind the play on words is a poignant truth. Everyone longs for peace in some way—whether it's a sense of inner peace and calm, respite from confrontation in the home or at work, a peaceful resolution to violent conflict on the national level, or all of the above. But we often spend our energy looking for peace in all the wrong places. Genuine peace is something that we cannot truly achieve without God. Only in turning away from sin and drawing close to God will we experience authentic, lasting peace within ourselves and among nations.

▶ Read DOCAT

Read nos. 270–283.

▶ What Does DOCAT Say?

1. What is the relationship between sin and peace?

2. How is Jesus the ultimate peacemaker?

3. Who has the duty to seek peace?

4. According to no. 274, what attitude is essential to spreading peace?

5. According to no. 275, what kind of peace is the goal of the Christian?

6. What is the first thing the Church does for peace?

▶ DO reflect

The Hebrew word for peace is "shalom." This peace is so much more than the absence of conflict or violence. It means a total well-being, what St. Augustine called the "tranquility of order": everything in its proper order and its proper state. The deepest sense of shalom (peace) is right relationship with God, the spiritual well-being that comes from living a life faithful to God's covenant.

Sin shatters our shalom. It puts everything out of order both within our souls and in our relationships with others and disrupts the tranquility of heart and mind that God wants to give us. In the Sacrament of Reconciliation, God draws us back to him in order to restore our shalom. By his grace we can be instruments of his peace in the world.

1. Do you like going to confession? Why or why not?

2. When is the last time you went to confession? How did you feel afterward?

3. Do you think you can have shalom in your relationships if you are not reconciled to God? Why or why not?

▶ What Does the Bible Say?

1. Read Ephesians 2:14. Why do you think St. Paul says that Jesus himself is our peace, rather than merely saying that he gives us peace? How might this difference be significant?

2. Look up Isaiah 2:2–4 and 11:6–9. What kind of peace is the Messiah expected to bring? What role will knowing and serving God have in bringing about this peace?

3. Read John 14:27 and 1 Peter 2:24. How does Christ offer us peace?

DO Chat

1. What kinds of things disrupt your inner peace? How does a lack of inner peace affect your interactions with others?

2. Have you ever had a hard time forgiving someone? If so, why was it hard? What helped you forgive them? If not, what do you think it is that makes it easier to forgive people?

3. Think of a time when someone has forgiven you. How did it feel to know you needed forgiveness? How did it feel to be forgiven?

DO Challenge

Resolve: Make a choice to forgive anyone against whom you might be holding a grudge, even if you feel like the person's words or actions are unforgivable.

Memorize: St. John of the Cross prayed, "O blessed Jesus, give me stillness of soul in you. Let your mighty calmness reign in me. Rule me, O King of Gentleness, King of Peace." Memorize this prayer.

Act: Go to confession this week.

NOTES

WAR AND PEACE

▶ Behind DOCAT

Mother Teresa once said, "If we have no peace, it is because we have forgotten that we belong to each other." From the earliest times, the story of humanity has been marked by violence. Beginning with Cain killing his brother Abel, mankind has resorted over and over again to aggression to get what it wants. Violence begets violence, leading to larger wars and bloodier revolutions. War may seem like an inevitable fact not only of history but also of the future, but the Church refuses to accept it as a "necessary" evil.

At the same time, every person has a right to act in defense of self and others. If someone is responsible for the lives of others, then defense isn't only a right but a serious responsibility. "You shall not kill" (Exodus 20:13) is a commandment against deliberately taking an innocent life, not against a legitimate defensive act that results in the death of the aggressor. While non-violent solutions are without exception preferable, self-defense and fighting in defense of one's country are not in conflict with the Christian's duty to strive for peace (cf. CCC, paragraphs 2263–2265).

▶ Read DOCAT

Read nos. 284–297.

▶ What Does DOCAT Say?

1. What does the Church say about war?
2. What rights do governments have when faced with violent aggression?
3. What is necessary for war to be avoided in the long-term?
4. How should sanctions be used?
5. What are the conditions for a just, defensive war?
6. What kind of orders do soldiers have an obligation to disobey?

DO reflect

In the Sermon on the Mount, Jesus takes several laws from the Old Covenant and applies them not only to a person's actions but also to his interior disposition. And so while the Law of Moses prohibited murder, Jesus tells his disciples that hating someone is like committing murder in one's heart. Now, most people can be angry at someone—even feel hatred—without coming close to plotting to kill the person. But God isn't concerned only with our actions; he's also concerned with the state of heart and mind that paves the way for the action. So Jesus calls us to an even higher standard: don't hate. Don't let anger fester in your heart (cf. Ephesians 4:26). If there is less hatred in our hearts, then there will be less violence in our world.

 Why do you think Jesus compares anger and hatred to murder?

 Do you think it does any damage to a person emotionally or spiritually to hold onto anger and hatred? Why or why not? Have you ever experienced negative effects from holding onto anger or hatred?

❸ What is the difference between hating someone and just disliking them? What are some ways to prevent dislike from turning into hatred?

▶ What Does the Bible Say?

1. Read Matthew 5:21–22 and 1 John 3:15. What does the New Covenant say about murder?

2. Look up Leviticus 24:17–21. What kind of response to violence did this law allow? How would this law affect the potential for escalating violence?

3. Look up Matthew 26:52 and Luke 6:29. What does Jesus say about responding to violence with violence?

DO Chat

1. Why do you think the Church sees a moral distinction between wars of aggression (or conquest) and fighting a war of self-defense?

2. Do you agree with St. John Paul II's description of war as a "defeat for humanity"? Why or why not?

3. What are some of the reasons that wars begin? Which of these reasons do you think would be easiest to prevent? Why?

DO Challenge

Pray: Take time every day this week to pray for wisdom and protection for your nation's military personnel.

Notice: If you know people who have served or are currently serving in the military, thank them for their service.

NOTES

▶ Behind DOCAT

New York City and Washington, D.C., September 11, 2001. Moscow, October 23, 2002. Madrid, March 11, 2004. London, July 7, 2005. Oslo, July 22, 2011. Nigeria, April 14, 2014. Paris, November 13, 2015. These are only a handful of the larger terrorist attacks in the first decade and a half of the twenty-first century. Terrorism—the use of violence or the threat of violence to coerce or intimidate others—is a particularly insidious attack against human dignity because those who utilize it often strike at civilians going about their everyday lives. It is a weapon of fear, but Scripture tells us that "perfect love casts out fear" (1 John 4:18). Even in the face of terrorism, the Church calls us to live lives of love and reconciliation.

▶ Read DOCAT

Read nos. 298–304.

▶ What Does DOCAT Say?

1. Can there be any justification for acts of terrorism?

2. What are the four ethical principles for research in the natural sciences?

▶ What Does the Bible Say?

1. Read Romans 12:17–21. How does St. Paul say we should react when we are victims of evil?

DO reflect

In the face of evil actions, it can be easy to forget that the person committing those acts are still human persons beloved by God. Terrorism is a cruel and unjust attack against humanity, but the terrorists behind it aren't the ultimate enemy. The greatest enemy is Satan, and our human opponents are his victims as well.

This doesn't mean that terrorists shouldn't be held accountable for their crimes—their actions are evil and the world needs to be protected from them. But as difficult as it may be, the people themselves need our prayers and forgiveness, not our hatred. As St. Paul says in his letter to the Ephesians, "For we are not contending against flesh and blood, but...against the spiritual hosts of wickedness" (Ephesians 6:12). Our battle against evil is first and foremost a spiritual battle, and for that we need the armor of God.

1 Read Ephesians 6:13–18. Which parts of this spiritual armor do you feel like you need the most in your daily life? Why?

2 Do you see a connection between physical violence and spiritual warfare? Do you think it makes any difference to view other people as victims of Satan's deceit rather than as the true enemy? Why or why not?

3 What can you do to try to respond with mercy rather than with anger and hatred when someone wrongs you in some way?

DO Chat

1. In what ways is terrorism different from other forms of war and violence?

2. Do you think that scientists should conduct research that has the potential to be used for evil as well as for good? Why or why not?

DO Challenge

Resolve: Choose to let go of any fear that is holding you back from loving others as God is calling you to love them. Ask for God's grace to help you be courageous in love.

Memorize: Memorize your favorite verse from Ephesians 6.

NOTES

NOTES

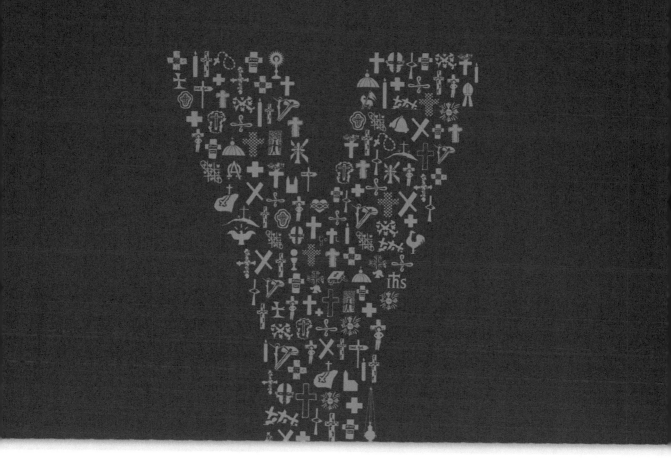

PART 12

PERSONAL AND SOCIETAL COMMITMENT: LOVE IN ACTION

▶ "for I was hungry and you gave me food, I was thirsty and you gave me drink, I was a stranger and you welcomed me, I was naked and you clothed me, I was sick and you visited me, I was in prison and you came to me."

—Matthew 25:35-36

TOPIC 1 | WE BELONG TOGETHER

▶ Behind DOCAT

Jesus calls his followers to change the world. That's a pretty tall order—there are innumerable problems in the world today, most of them far too big for any one person to make a difference. But God hasn't called us to undertake this imposing task by ourselves. When we are baptized, we enter into the Church: the family of God, a community of faith, and the very Body of Christ. It is as members of this Body that we are sent out into the world to transform it. We don't have to do it alone, nor can we do it alone. But united in faith, hope, and charity, we can truly move mountains.

▶ Read DOCAT

Read nos. 305–314.

▶ What Does DOCAT Say?

1. What is central to a Christian way of living together?

2. What motivates the Christian to be socially involved?

3. According to no. 311 what two things does the Church give us to strengthen and sustain us?

4. What do clergy do for the faithful that the laity cannot do for themselves?

▶ DO reflect

In several of his letters, St. Paul describes the Church as the Body of Christ (*cf.* Romans 12:4–5; 1 Corinthians 12:12–31; Ephesians 1:23; Colossians 1:18, 24). This is more than just a metaphor; it is the metaphysical reality of the real unity between every baptized Christian and Jesus Christ. And if each believer is really and truly united to Christ, then every Christian is also really and truly united to every other Christian. This unity extends not only to the rest of the Church on earth (the Church Militant) but also to all the saints in Heaven (the Church Triumphant) and the faithful in Purgatory (the Church Suffering). This journey to Heaven, marked as it is with the mission to be salt and light to a troubled world, is one that we make together. As the letter to the Hebrews reminds us, "Therefore, since we are surrounded by so great a cloud of witnesses, let us also lay aside every weight, and sin which clings so closely, and let us run with perseverance the race that is set before us" (Hebrews 12:1).

1. Who is your favorite saint? Why?

2. St. Paul explains that just as different body parts have different functions, so also different Christians are called to do different things for the good of the Church. Which part of the body do you associate with what you feel God is calling you to do at this point in your life? Why?

▶ What Does the Bible Say?

1. Read Matthew 25:35–40. What does this passage tell us about what it means to serve God?

2. According to Matthew 25:44–45, when we fail to care for those in need, whom are we really failing?

3. Look up Matthew 5:13–16. According to Jesus's words here, is there any such thing as a "private" faith as a Christian?

4. Read Mark 16:15–16. What responsibility do Christians have to "the whole creation"?

DO Chat

1. Do you think that someone can fully follow Christ without being part of the Church he founded? Why or why not?

2. What are some things that Christians can do to be the "salt of the earth" (Matthew 5:13) and the "light of the world" (Matthew 5:14)? What things cause Christians to lose taste or be hidden under a bushel?

DO Challenge

Resolve: Look for one way that God is calling you to be salt or light in your everyday life. Pray for the grace to live your faith courageously in that situation.

NOTES

▶ Behind DOCAT

Many people wonder when the Church is going to "get with the times." The world is a very different place today than it was 2,000 years ago, and it's about time the Church caught up with all of the changes. But "different" doesn't automatically mean "better"— that's the myth of progress—and this expectation misunderstands the fundamental mission of the Church to "carry forward the work of Christ" *(Gaudium et Spes,* 3). The Church goes where God sends her, whether or not the world approves.

The Second Vatican Council said that the Church has "the duty of scrutinizing the signs of the times and of interpreting them in the light of the Gospel." This duty is misunderstood by some to mean that the Church needs to understand the modern world in order to conform to it, but the real duty is to understand the world in order to figure out how to best present the unchanging truth of the Gospel. The Church measures the world by the truth of the Gospel, not the Gospel by the state of the world. This unyielding dedication to the truth often places Christians in difficult and unpopular positions, but this is exactly what Jesus told his disciples to expect.

▶ Read DOCAT

Read nos. 315–323.

DO reflect

When God brought the Israelites out of slavery in Egypt, he gave them laws to make them different from other nations. After 400 years there, the Israelites had absorbed much of Egypt's religion and culture; it was one thing to get Israel out of Egypt but it was quite another to get Egypt out of Israel. The purpose of the many laws concerning what to eat and how to wash and what was clean and unclean were all meant to keep Israel from assimilating pagan cultures as they had in Egypt. The laws helped Israel be in the world but not of it.

In the New Covenant, God hasn't given his Church the same kinds of laws to keep us separate from unbelievers, but we face the same dangers of assimilation. We are called to go out into the world to share the Good News of God's love, but we must take care that we do not let ourselves be conformed to the world. This isn't always easy, and sometimes it might seem tempting just to lock ourselves away so we don't have to deal with the influence of the world. But with the grace of the sacraments, the guidance of Sacred Scripture, and the support and encouragement of fellow Christians, we can live out St. Paul's exhortation: "Do not be conformed to this world but be transformed by the renewal of your mind, that you may prove what is the will of God, what is good and acceptable and perfect" (Romans 12:2).

 Do you feel it is challenging to resist being conformed to the modern world? Why or why not?

 What do you do to prevent the world from having more influence over your life than God does?

▶ What Does DOCAT Say?

1. What is the most important book for Christians? What other resources are important for understanding the faith?

2. What things cannot be changed in Church teaching? In what ways can Church teaching change with the changing times?

3. What are some prerequisites for responsible involvement with a political party?

4. What are three prerequisites for involvement with a non-Christian organization?

▶ What Does the Bible Say?

1. What does Matthew 18:20 say about the importance of gathering together in community as Christians?

2. Jeremiah 29:7 is an instruction for the Jews living in exile in Babylon. How can Christians apply this instruction as true citizens of Heaven living now in this earthly city?

3. What does Psalm 119:105 say about the Word of God? What does Psalm 1:2 say we should do with the Word of God?

4. What does Jesus tell his disciples to expect from the world in John 15:18–21?

DO Chat

1. Do you ever feel lonely in your commitment to Christ? Why or why not? What resources do you have available to give you a sense of community with other Christians?

2. How important is Sacred Scripture to you personally? Why?

3. When have you had the strongest sense of belonging and commitment to the Church? What facilitated that experience?

DO Challenge

Memorize: Memorize Psalm 119:105.

Read: Spend 10 minutes reading Scripture every day this week.

NOTES

▶ Behind DOCAT

In the Nicene Creed we recite at Mass, we proclaim faith in the "one, holy, catholic, and apostolic Church." This Church sometimes seems like a bit of a paradox, because while we acknowledge that "all have sinned and fall short of the glory of God" (Romans 3:23), we also recognize that "the Church...is held, as a matter of faith, to be unfailingly holy" *(Lumen Gentium,* 39). So we have a perfectly holy Church made up of very imperfect people.

This is good news for us! After all, Jesus came "not to call the righteous, but sinners" (Mark 2:17). But the Church would not do us much good if it were only as holy as its earthly members. Rather, the Church has Christ's own holiness and therefore is able to offer us the path to holiness.

It is important to keep in mind the distinction between the Church as a whole and the individual members of the Church. When we are faced with another Christian—especially a leader in the Church—who fails us or disappoints us, we must remember that that person is someone in need of grace just as we are. But we can always place our full trust in Christ's Church, and we will never be disappointed or led astray.

▶ Read DOCAT

Read nos. 324–328.

▶ What Does DOCAT Say?

1. What are some criteria for appropriate or constructive argument within the Church?

2. According to no. 327, what is necessary for authentic interreligious (ecumenical) encounters?

DO reflect

Do you ever wonder about Jesus's second coming and the end of the world? Sometimes it seems like there is so much wrong with the world that it would just be better for Christ to come back and end it all.

Scripture offers a different approach to our prayerful anticipation of Christ's return in glory. In Revelation, St. John receives a vision of the heavenly wedding feast of the Lamb of God and his Bride, the Church. The key moment for this triumphal marriage at the end of time is not when the groom is ready—it's when the bride is finally ready. Revelation 19:7–8 says, "'Let us rejoice and exult and give [God] the glory, for the marriage of the Lamb has come, and his Bride has made herself ready; it was granted her to be clothed with fine linen, bright and pure'—for the fine linen is the righteous deeds of the saints." Maybe we don't have to wait for things to get worse before Jesus returns—we are supposed to be preparing the Church for the end of time by our acts of love. The Bride is already made holy, but for the heavenly wedding feast she must be clothed in the righteous deeds of her members.

1. What are some "righteous deeds of the saints" that you are aware of (past or present)? How do these kinds of actions make the holiness of the Church more evident?

2. How do you think about your relationship with the Church? What, if anything, do you think the Church needs from you?

▶ What Does the Bible Say?

1. Read Luke 10:16. According to this verse, how are we to view the authority of the clergy?

2. What does 1 Peter 5:1–7 say about how Church leaders should exercise their authority and how laity should respond?

3. According to John 17:20–23 and Ephesians 4:4–6, what is the source of Christian unity?

DO Chat

1. What do you think are appropriate ways to criticize the Church? What are inappropriate ways to criticize the Church? Why?

2. What kinds of encounters have you had with people of other faiths? What was positive about these interactions? What was negative?

3. What do you think is important when interacting with people of other faiths? Why?

DO Challenge

Pray: Pray for the pope, your bishop, and your pastor this week, that God would help them live up to the exhortation of 1 Peter 5.

Resolve: Make a list of "righteous deeds" of love that you will do throughout the week to add to the fine linen of the Bride of the Lamb.

NOTES

NOTES

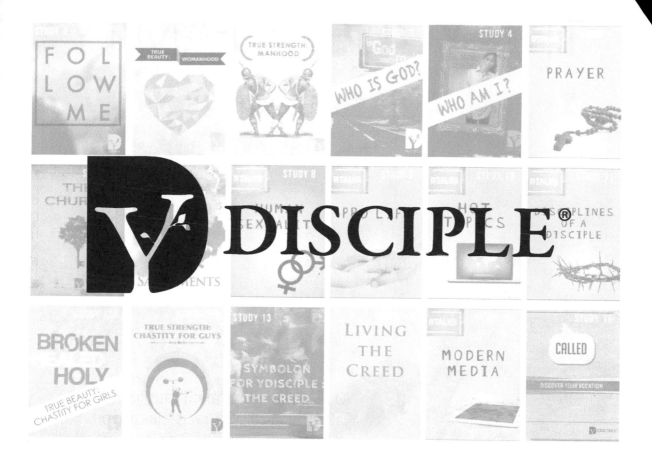

THE **YOUCAT** FAMILY

YOUCAT is short for Youth Catechism of the Catholic Church, which was launched on World Youth Day, 2011. Developed with the help of young Catholics and written for high-school age people and young adults, YOUCAT is an accessible, contemporary expression of the Catholic Faith. The appealing graphic format includes Questions-and-Answers, highly-readable commentary, summary definitions of key terms, Bible citations and inspiring and thought-provoking quotes from Saints and others in the margins. What's more, YOUCAT is keyed to the Catechism of the Catholic Church, so people can go deeper.